"If you don't plan to sit by the fire all winter, but rather want to get out and enjoy the snow and the cold, *Winter Hiking and Camping* should be at the top of your list. . . .Even if you're an experienced cold-weather camper, you'll probably find quite a few tips on how to make your next trip to the snow backcountry a more pleasurable experience."

—*Cheyenne* (Wyoming) *Eagle-Tribune*

"Following [Lanza's] guidelines, you can expect to stay safe, warm, and comfortable. . . .If camping or hiking in the winter sounds way too scary, this book should help chase off a few fears. Using the techniques in this book will make a huge difference."

—*Idaho Falls Post Register*

"This book could be the equivalent of a snowplow in the backwoods—able to open up new avenues with tips, tricks, and must-know safety techniques."

—*Erie* (PA) *Times*

"*Winter Hiking & Camping* makes a good case to enjoy the outdoors in winter."

—*Deseret Morning News*

"This will give newbies a good base on winter backcountry use, whether they camp or not."

—*Billings Gazette*

"Good to have for those who travel a lot in the winter months in snow country."

—*Klamath Falls Herald and News*

Winter Hiking & Camping

MANAGING
COLD FOR
**COMFORT
& SAFETY**

Michael Lanza

THE MOUNTAINEERS BOOKS

Published by
The Mountaineers Books
1001 SW Klickitat Way, Suite 201
Seattle, WA 98134

The Mountaineers Books is the nonprofit publishing arm of The Mountaineers Club, an organization founded in 1906 and dedicated to the exploration, preservation, and enjoyment of outdoor and wilderness areas.

BACKPACKER
THE OUTDOORS AT YOUR DOORSTEP

33 East Minor Street
Emmaus, PA 18098

Published simultaneously in Great Britain by Cordee, 3a DeMontfort Street, Leicester, England, LE1 7HD
Manufactured in the United States of America

Project Editor/Copy Editor: Dottie Martin
Cover and Book Designer: The Mountaineers Books
Layout Artist: Mayumi Thompson
Illustrators: Hans J. Neuhart, Brian D. Metz, and Jennifer LaRock Shontz
All photographs by the author unless otherwise noted.

Cover photograph: © Rob Bossi
Frontispiece: *Snowshoeing up Freeman Peak, Boise National Forest, Idaho*

Library of Congress Cataloging-in-Publication Data
Lanza, Michael A., 1961-
  Backpacker magazine winter hiking & camping : managing cold for comfort & safety / Michael Lanza.— 1st ed.
      p. cm. — (Backpacker magazine series)
Includes bibliographical references (p.   ) and index.
  ISBN 0-89886-947-1
  1. Snow camping. 2. Snow camping—Equipment and supplies. 3. Hiking.
4. Hiking—Equipment and supplies. I. Backpacker. II. Title. III.Series.
  GV198.9.L36 2003
  796.54—dc21
                                        2003010866

♻ Printed on recycled paper
ISBN 10: 0-89886-947-1
ISBN 13: 978-0-89886-947-7

Contents

Preface

The Tao of Cold

That you have picked up and opened this book, even if tentatively, is a bold first step. You have begun the journey. You already have an inkling of a truth that I will confirm for you now: *Cold is your friend.* Do not shrink away from it. Embrace it. When the temperature passes stealthily through that magical threshold of thirty-two degrees Fahrenheit, or zero degrees Celsius, it opens doors for us into a new realm.

This revelation does not come easily to us humans, who must compensate for our inadequate natural defenses against the cold by donning artificial skin and fat merely to survive. We don't have the fur of polar bears or the blubber of seals. Yet, we have lived in middle and upper latitudes around the world—places with winter—for thousands of years. We've learned not only how to survive in cold environments but how to thrive in and enjoy them.

Why even hike and camp in winter? Granted, it's an acquired taste. And the very need to ask some questions precludes an easy answer. The pleasures of winter are at once tricky to convey to the uninitiated and self-explanatory to the participant. The joys of winter hiking and camping are spectacular, subtle, and sometimes elusive. Few silences are as complete as a windless landscape stilled by a thick comforter of snow. An ice- and snow-covered mountaintop above tree line will forever redefine "white" in your mind. The low, cool light of sunny winter days throws almost perpetual long shadows, lending the natural world a sharpness and contrast that you won't see on summer days when the high sun bleaches everything flat.

I referred earlier to the temperature at which water freezes in part because the book you hold addresses the outdoor world in its frozen state—mostly, anyway. Put on a warm hat, because much of what follows in these pages will take place below freezing—or just barely above it. This book ostensibly offers advice on what to do and what *not* to do when hiking and camping in the backcountry in winter. However, in reality, the skills transmitted are relevant in any season and environment where snow, sleet, freezing rain, or just-plain-cold rain may fall and where temperatures may swing wildly from just above freezing to well below freezing. This book makes frequent reference to "winter hiking," although in many places, you'll often be on snowshoes or touring skis. Chapter 2 covers these modes of transportation.

Across the breadth of climates, latitudes, and elevation ranges that exist in the United States, winter exhibits a multitude of personalities, sometimes resembling spring and fall—and occasionally, in select places, making cameo appearances in summer. Learn to recognize and coexist peacefully with those many faces of winter, and you will possess knowledge and skills directly applicable to heading into many mountain ranges in spring or autumn or climbing a high peak in any month. Developing winter skills is basically just adding layers of sophistication to your three-season hiking and camping skills—earning a master's degree in deeper cold on top of your three-season bachelor's degree. Once you've earned it, the calendar will no longer limit your outdoor adventures.

If your interest lies only in hiking in winter, but not in sleeping outside overnight, you may think Part II of this book is irrelevant to you. I hope you rethink that position. Day hiking in the summer, especially on an all-day outing that takes you miles from any road, requires a certain degree of preparedness for emergencies: carrying extra food, clothing, and water, for instance. Get benighted in summer, and you may spend an uncomfortable night outside—but you won't likely freeze to death. The winter day-tripper, though, must accept a hard truth about this game: Accidents happen—the winter environment arguably presents more risks and more opportunity for accidents than does summer—and spending an unplanned night outside in winter without being prepared for it could, to put it delicately, conclude your winter hiking career. On a winter hike that will take you far from roads, especially a relatively difficult hike, you *must* be ready for the worst—being stranded outside for the night—and know how to get through it safely. Even if you never plan to sleep outside in winter—or at least, not deliberately—the information in Part II is as relevant to you as your own beating heart.

There's another, deeper reason I opened this Preface talking about the temperature at which water freezes. The transformation of water from liquid to solid is a metaphor for the transcendence we achieve with that first step toward seeing winter as an invitation rather than a rejection. The real, underlying agenda behind this book is to convince you that, in many ways, temperatures below freezing (or moderate temperatures below freezing) make heading into the backcountry *easier.* Many experienced four-season outdoor adventurers will tell you the ideal temperature for moving through the backcountry is in the low to mid-twenties Fahrenheit: If dressed properly, you won't perspire too heavily, yet it's not so cold that you're uncomfortable or at risk of losing fingers or toes, plus there's no danger of getting wet because everything's frozen. Modern technical clothing and gear make getting outside in winter a relatively comfortable experience. Then, of course, there's another significant benefit of winter hiking and camping: no bugs.

Indeed, once you have shed the self-limiting negative bias toward winter that many of us harbor, you realize that, in many ways, winter is a more inviting time of year to venture into the forests and mountains than summer—that cold is your friend. Marry that attitude to the skills you glean from this book, and you'll have the business of heading into the backcountry in deep cold down . . . cold.

Michael Lanza

A Note About Safety

Safety is an important concern in all outdoor activities. No book can alert you to every hazard or anticipate the limitations of every reader. The descriptions of techniques and procedures in this book are intended to provide general information. Nothing substitutes for formal instruction, routine practice, and plenty of experience. When you follow any of the procedures described here, you assume responsibility for your own safety. Use this book as a general guide to further information. Under normal conditions, excursions into the backcountry require attention to traffic, road and trail conditions, weather, terrain, the capabilities of your party, and other factors. Keeping informed on current conditions and exercising common sense are the keys to a safe, enjoyable outing.

The Mountaineers Books

Introduction

Y ou no doubt know the phrases "leave no trace" and "take only pictures; leave only footprints." We know those slogans thanks to an effort that has led to much of the American backcountry suffering less abuse from human use than it did up until the late 1970s and 1980s. The Leave No Trace educational program and guidelines put together by a partnership of the National Outdoor Leadership School (NOLS) in Lander, Wyoming, the U.S. Forest Service, Bureau of Land Management, National Park Service, and U.S. Fish and Wildlife Service was chartered in 1991. NOLS administers the program and spearheads the educational effort through a nonprofit organization that also carries the name Leave No Trace, Inc., or LNT. LNT consists of seven basic principles, along with a standard curriculum for land managers and educators. Each of us who hike today without seeing discarded candy wrappers, unsightly fire rings, improperly dug cat holes, or backpackers washing pots and pans in a lake or leaving a water-runoff trench around their tent has benefited from this ethic and effort.

To keep our most-cherished places beautiful, we must contribute to the responsible stewardship of the land. The LNT principles provide guidelines for minimizing our physical impact on the fragile environments where we hike. These guidelines leave some room for interpretation because it's impossible to create specific rules for every possible situation encountered in the backcountry.

The following are the LNT principles:
1. Plan ahead and prepare.
2. Travel and camp on durable surfaces.
3. Dispose of waste properly.
4. Leave what you find.
5. Minimize impact of campfires.
6. Respect wildlife.
7. Be considerate of other visitors.

How do you, as a conscientious hiker, apply these guidelines to your own behavior? First, by simply keeping the principles in mind—not necessarily memorizing them, but thinking about what they mean and how to use them when you're on the trail. Pack out all trash, even biodegradable items such as orange and banana peels, at any time of year—without exception. If the food waste isn't native to the environment you're in, it doesn't belong there. Trash attracts scavengers, many of which chase away native species and begin to associate people with food.

Where snow does not cover the ground, follow the trail and avoid shortcuts. Walk on durable surfaces—gravel, sand, rock, snow, dry alpine meadows, and grasslands. Look at what your sole does to the ground. On a packed-dirt trail, chances are you won't see your boot print. However, on wet trails or tundra, or off-trail, every step can leave an unsightly gash. In those places, step on rocks, soil, or vegetation that isn't sensitive to footsteps. If you see an unmarked, dirt trail, use it; otherwise try not to walk where other people have stepped. Avoid cutting into sidehills; if your treads expose fresh dirt, seek tougher ground. Be even more careful along streambanks and in other erosion-prone areas. In a group, walk single file on trails, but spread out when hiking cross-country.

When camping in the backcountry, follow the land managers' guidelines for camping. If there aren't regulations or designated campsites, your first choice should be a well-established site, where ground vegetation is worn away but decomposing leaves and needles are still present in spots. Don't camp in sites where prior use is only slightly noticeable (flattened grass and leaves, scattered charcoal). If there are no well-established sites, camp in a spot that shows no signs of prior use. Never rearrange the landscape to suit your needs. Camp out of view of the main trail and at least 200 feet from water sources.

Where snow does cover the ground, walk and camp on snow whenever possible; a base of at least two feet of snow is recommended for a campsite. Plan and prepare well for your outing—spending an unintended night outside is not only uncomfortable and potentially dangerous in winter but you may inadvertently be forced to camp someplace where your presence will leave a mark on the environment. Plan to cook with a stove; check the legality of campfires before assuming you can build one; and if you build one, disperse it completely after it's out. Spells of warm weather in winter and spring accelerate the melting of snow, often leaving long stretches of trail wet and muddy and therefore more susceptible to erosion exacerbated by hikers than at any other time; avoid hitting the trail during those times.

Wildlife is especially vulnerable during winter, when food sources become scarce and animals must conserve energy to maintain sufficient stores of fat to survive through spring. Do nothing to harass wildlife—this includes approaching them closely enough to cause them to move away. Stay away from obvious nesting sites and dens, and from young animals.

Disposal of human waste gets particularly tricky wherever snow covers the ground thickly. It's easy to think that the snow and freezing temperatures give you license to go anywhere. But think of it this way: The solid waste you leave, even if buried under snow, will not decompose until the snow begins melting away weeks or months after your visit. Runoff from snowmelt can carry that waste into creeks and streams. At the least, some hiker may come along to find your deposit lying on bare ground.

Use trailhead and backcountry toilets whenever available. Otherwise, as at any other time of year, urinate and defecate at least 200 feet from any water source. Do your business as far from trails and established campsites as possible and away from low areas where water runs off in spring. The recommended place for defecating is at the base of a tree: Dig a hole in the snow at the trunk. If you can, get down to and into the ground. But even if you can't reach the ground, burying solid waste in snow at the base of a tree ensures that solar radiation coming off the tree will cause the waste to decompose more quickly than if buried in snow in open terrain. If a tree is not available, find a large boulder. In addition, don't bury toilet paper; instead, pack it out.

How to Use This Book

This book is divided into two parts. Part I (Chapters 1 through 6) covers everything you need to know to hike, snowshoe, or ski tour in the backcountry in freezing temperatures. (Technical climbing and telemark skiing are not covered; see the Bibliography in Appendix B for titles in those subjects.) The skills covered here are relevant beyond winter, useful in any season and environment where snow, sleet, freezing rain, or cold rain may fall and where temperatures may vary greatly. Part I instructs you in managing cold for comfort, enjoyment, and safety and avoiding environmental hazards.

Part II (Chapters 7 through 10) covers winter camping. Although this part is shorter than Part I, that does not mean that the information is less valuable; consider Part II an addendum to Part I, or a second-level course to build on the skills covered in Part I. It does not rehash the material covered in Part I but merely expands on it for readers who plan to winter camp or who want to be prepared to spend (that is, *survive*) an unplanned night outside in an emergency. Beyond the day-hiking skills and equipment covered in Part I, this part covers what you need to know to sleep outside in freezing temperatures. Winter campers—or three-season backpackers seeking to develop their skills at camping in temperatures below freezing—should read both parts. Winter hikers (including those on snowshoes or skis) should read Part II as well.

Throughout the text, select terms appear in boldface type; see the Glossary in Appendix C for additional explanation of these terms.

One Last Thing . . .

As you become a seasoned hiker, you'll come to recognize and appreciate the hard labor that goes into maintaining thousands of miles of trails across the country.

Much of that work, even on public lands, is done by volunteer trail maintenance crews, nonprofit conservation organizations, and hiking clubs such as those listed in Appendix A. These groups do good work and are always in need of support—both in the form of money and volunteer hours. Join an organization in your area; support the group that maintains your favorite hiking destination. Help out in any way you can—it's almost as satisfying as hiking.

We're interested in your feedback about this book's content and presentation so that we can improve it with each future edition. Send your comments to The Mountaineers Books, 1001 SW Klickitat Way, Suite 201, Seattle, WA 98134. Visit the website of The Mountaineers Books at *www.mountaineersbooks.org* or the website of *Backpacker* magazine at *www.backpacker.com*.

PART I
Winter Hiking

Chapter 1

Where to Go

You are a spring-through-autumn day hiker. Perhaps you're even an avid, experienced three-season hiker. Maybe a backpacker or a climber. I make this speculation confidently because—like me and many other winter outdoor enthusiasts—most people who begin to explore the backcountry in the colder months have already logged many a day outdoors in the warmer months. As I mentioned in the Preface, the ability to appreciate and revel in winter is something of an acquired taste.

If you've been hiking for some time, you've probably read guidebooks, gotten familiar with trails and peaks in your area, and joined a hiking club or have other connections in the broader hiking community. You know where to go, in other words. As you look for destinations for your winter adventures, you'll use many of the same resources that you use during the other seasons and even go to many of the same places. You'll find that potential destinations are as plentiful, or nearly so, as in summer and fall. Many of the same trails are accessible in winter. Public lands such as municipal parks and state and national parks and forests usually keep their trails open year-round, although getting to them may be a bigger challenge than getting around on them. Some states operate Park 'n' Ski (or similarly named) areas

◀ A winter hiker gets enthusiastic about snowshoeing up Freeman Peak in Idaho's Boise National Forest.

on public land where, for a nominal fee, you can park in a plowed trailhead lot and access trails maintained for ski touring, snowshoeing, or hiking. You may even have more potential winter destinations if you live where some roads that are open to motor vehicles in the warm months are not plowed in winter but are open to ski tourers or snowshoers.

Can I Get There?

You'll have to evaluate your winter destination choices from a different perspective, with, in many ways, a more discerning eye. For starters, road access may change: The same road you drive easily in summer may be closed, not routinely plowed, not passable to a low-clearance vehicle or a vehicle lacking tire chains, or only partially plowed to the trailhead—meaning you'll have to travel the remaining distance to the trailhead on foot. Weather may prevent you from getting to the trailhead or may be so severe that you end your hike before beginning it. In addition, the weather at the trailhead in a mountain region will usually be colder and potentially stormier than in the valley where you got into your car. Some public lands such as national parks may close for brief periods at the beginning or end of winter for management reasons (such as clearing snow from unplowed roads). The trails themselves will, of course, be in a different condition than you're accustomed to in summer and fall, but we'll cover that later.

In short, almost wherever you live, you can probably expect to enjoy nearly as much access to trails in winter as you do in summer. However, make no assumptions about what you'll run into either getting to the trailhead or once on the trail. Do some research and planning. Call the management agency or appropriate organization (in some areas it may be a hiking club) or check its website for information. If needed, purchase tire chains for your vehicle and practice putting them on the tires on a nice day at home before you have to put them on with numb fingers in a raging blizzard. The following questions should be answered before driving to the trailhead:

- ▲ Is the road maintained all the way to the trailhead in winter?
- ▲ If not, how far from the trailhead is the road plowed, and is there a place to park?
- ▲ Has it been plowed since the last snowstorm?
- ▲ Might the road's condition potentially require a high-clearance vehicle or tire chains?
- ▲ Is the trail popular in winter or rarely used?
- ▲ How much snow, if any, is likely to be on the trail, and is the snow packed firm, or is it light and deep (see Chapter 4)?
- ▲ Is there likely to be a path broken through the snow by previous hikers, skiers, or snowshoers, or should you expect to be breaking fresh trail (see Popular Vs. Little-Used Trails)?
- ▲ What's the weather forecast for the area (see Chapter 5)?

Popular Vs. Little-Used Trails

In New Hampshire's White Mountains, the Old Bridle Path and Greenleaf Trail provide a direct 4-mile route to the summit of Mount Lafayette, a popular 4000-footer year-round. In winter, although it can be severely cold and windy on the mountain—indeed, even at the trailhead in Franconia Notch—a veritable parade of hikers ensures a packed trough through the snow from the trailhead to the alpine zone (where the wind doesn't let much snow accumulate, anyway). By mid-morning the day after a fresh snowfall, hikers often won't need snowshoes, and the walking is relatively fast on the packed snow.

However, just a few minutes' drive south of that trailhead, the Flume Slide Trail up another 4000-footer, Mount Flume, sees little foot traffic in winter—the trail is steep and exposed, and the summit of Flume is less popular year-round than Lafayette, which is higher. A few years ago, I climbed Flume on a beautiful March day, when there hadn't been a new snowfall in many days to cover up any old tracks, yet I saw no human tracks at all. I had trouble just following the trail, lost it for a time, and literally saw no one the entire climb.

The lesson is obvious: Even in the popular White Mountains, accessible to millions of people, you'll find a dichotomy of experience between hiking, snowshoeing, or skiing a popular winter trail and one that receives little use. This is true in many places throughout the country in winter. As you look for trails and routes to break in your winter boots, think about the type of experience you'd like and how it will be served or impeded by a trail's or peak's popularity. The trade-offs between the relative solitude of a little-used trail vs. the relative safety in numbers

Skiers on the popular Zealand Trail in New Hampshire's White Mountain National Forest

on a popular trail get magnified in winter, when safety becomes doubly important, while solitude remains, for many, a desirable quality—and it's conceivable that you may not see anyone for days on a remote trail in winter.

Novice winter hikers, snowshoers, and skiers may want to cut their teeth on relatively popular routes, where it's less likely that they'll get lost or be slowed by breaking trails through untracked snow (see Chapter 4) and where the presence of other people provides a greater margin of safety by virtue of potentially having more people available to help in an emergency. That's not to say that hitting the trail in winter is inherently safer when there are more people around—the hazards don't disappear, including the potential for losing the trail if, for instance, strong gusts cause snow to drift over the trough packed out by others before you or if whomever broke trail through the fresh snow ahead of you took a wrong turn. You still have to stay on your toes. Nevertheless, having others around probably lowers the probability of making certain mistakes, and having extra help if you do get into trouble certainly improves your odds of getting to civilization safely.

As you gain experience in winter hiking, and confidence in your ability to find your way in winter and your skill at staying warm in the cold, you might decide to seek the greater adventure of little-used trails or to venture off-trail (see Chapter 4). The enhanced difficulty and challenges will test you mentally and physically more than popular trails, but the satisfaction derived from being more self-sufficient and enjoying the solitude you find there—especially in winter—justify the added risk in the eyes of many. Just remember that self-reliance means just that: You and your companions have to be prepared to get yourselves out of any situation without expecting help to arrive. Remember also that experience gained in one winter environment doesn't always translate directly to another winter environment.

Guidebooks and Maps

As in summer and fall, guidebooks and maps are your primary source of detailed, on-the-ground information about your route in winter. However, be aware of their shortcomings. Guidebooks are generally written for hiking from spring through fall—although some better guidebooks contain information about the route in winter, especially if it's popular at that time of year. A guidebook that wasn't published or updated with a new edition in recent years may have inaccurate, outdated information.

Maps show terrain at ground level, not as it appears under several feet of snow or with a huge cornice overhanging a mountain pass. Additionally, some U.S. Geological Survey (USGS) topographic maps are decades old and inaccurate on the location of trails or do not show all the trails in a region. Winter has a habit of burying trails under deep snow or rendering mountain passes impassable. Winter erects obstacles such as icy cascades on a section of steep trail, a lot of blow downs, and deep drifts that force you to leave the trail—even if only temporarily—and find another way. Many commercial maps made for hiking and backpacking are on a scale of anywhere from 1:48,000 to 1:100,000 or higher, which simply does not show adequate detail for the routefinding dilemmas that frequently arise in winter. For this reason—especially on trails and routes that receive little human traffic in winter—detailed maps such as the 7.5-minute USGS quads in 1:24,000 scale are essential for reading the landscape when winter blows you off the trail. (See more about using maps and a compass in Chapter 4.)

Still, the map remains indispensable and a good guidebook can be useful for planning a winter outing, if it provides some description of the terrain, such as obstacles like river crossings (which may be unthinkable to attempt in winter temperatures) or steep, treeless slopes that could pose avalanche hazard. Consider the guidebook one source of information about the route in winter but not the only source. The best source of current information is someone who's been on the same trail recently or at least at the same time of year in the past; you might find someone such as this through a hiking club or its website, perhaps among your own friends and acquaintances, or possibly among the employees at a local outdoor gear store. New computer mapping software and online services let you create customized maps with your own notes about campsites or other noteworthy places along your route. Call the management agency for current information, but be sure to ask for a backcountry ranger or someone who actually goes into the backcountry in winter. Keep in mind that different sources of information may provide you with conflicting details—such as the distance from point A to point B—and you'll have to use your skills to determine the correct answer, as well as be prepared for dealing with whatever you encounter once you're actually there.

Permits and Regulations

Public lands that require a permit for overnight use or for a daytime visit from spring through fall usually enforce that rule through winter. U.S. national parks, for example, require a permit for camping in the backcountry at any time of year, including winter, and the parks limit the number of people sleeping in the backcountry. The difference is that demand for winter backcountry permits is much less than for permits in summer; therefore, you usually don't need to reserve a permit. Even in world-famous Yellowstone, I've walked into a backcountry ranger office right before multi-day winter trips and walked out with the necessary permit, without having reserved it beforehand.

Regulations on public lands sometimes vary in winter from the warmer months to protect flora or fauna. Restrictions on camping in summer and fall, for instance, may be relaxed in winter, when the ground is covered with snow. A management agency may provide winter backcountry travelers with a completely different set of regulations and recommendations than it provides to summer backpackers. Some parks, especially state lands, lack the funding to provide staff on-site through the

Taking in the view on Pilot Peak in Idaho's Boise National Forest

winter, which may translate to limitations on public access or merely no available services. Finding out a park's status in winter, and what the land managers advise and require, should be part of the preparation for any winter hike.

Permits and regulations can sometimes seem inconvenient and oppressive, and you may not always agree with them. However, they exist to manage a natural resource to maximize our enjoyment and minimize our impact. By respecting the rules at all times of year, we ensure that special places remain special.

Deciding Where to Go

Earlier in this chapter you read a list of several questions to consider before heading out to a chosen trail in winter. The information sought through those questions will tell you something about your destination. The other critical factors in the formula used in deciding where to go are you and your companions. With winter's beauty comes challenges both physical and mental that may exceed what you've encountered in summer or fall. A sunny, calm, relatively "warm" winter day is not too hard on the psyche; but turn down the outdoor thermostat ten or twenty degrees, and throw in strong, howling, icy wind and heavy snowfall under a leaden sky, and you may find yourself thinking, with some trepidation, "Do I belong out here?" Just as well, what's "comfortable" for one intrepid winter adventurer may seem downright threatening and dangerous to someone with a different experience base—and could be dangerous for someone who lacks the skills to handle the situation.

When heading out on a hike in August, you may not give more than a passing thought to whether something will happen that day that causes you to reflect on the goals you haven't yet accomplished in your life. But the harshness of the winter environment can do that. Slow, arduous terrain and severe winter weather have an amazing capacity for draining one's energy and confidence and inspiring an overwhelming nervousness; they make it harder to keep your wits about you and make good, safe decisions. I don't say this to dissuade you from hitting the trails in winter—just to make you pay more attention to your plans to avoid wrestling with deep thoughts about your own mortality. Winter demands that you think about where you're going, the potential weather, difficulty of the terrain, and on-the-ground snow and ice conditions and whether you're physically and mentally ready—and, more importantly, whether everyone in your party is ready, because the group always moves at the pace of its slowest member.

When planning a hike in any season, you already consider factors such as the planned mileage and elevation gain and loss of the trip, the relative difficulty of the trail and steepness of the terrain, and the maximum elevation you'll reach. Winter's cold, potential for severe storms, and the presence of snow and ice on the ground broaden the list of variables. Consider these additional questions (see Chapter 4 for gauging how far to go in winter conditions):

▲ Might the terrain be steeper and more exposed or the snow or ice conditions more difficult than you or anyone else in your group have handled in the past?

▲ Does your intended route stay within the relative protection of the forest or venture into open terrain, such as above tree line, where the weather can be much more severe?

▲ What's the forecast and potential for encountering conditions more severe—colder, windier, or with heavier precipitation—than you or anyone else have had to deal with before?

▲ If this trip becomes more difficult than anything you've previously done, are you all ready for it?

In evaluating your responses to those questions, take into account your fitness and that of everyone involved and everyone's emotional comfort level with things such as snow-covered slopes or freezing winds that are strong enough to knock you off balance. Lacking the stamina for the physical demands of the day will at a minimum slow you down, and exhaustion can lead to worse problems such as poor decision-making and injury. Snow slopes and strong winds aren't necessarily impediments to foot travel—unless one member of the party is uncomfortable with crossing a snow slope or unhinged by howling, frigid mountain winds. Then you might be slowed drastically. In short, the same hike you do in summer might be beyond your abilities in winter.

Winter presents a greater range between "easy" and "hard" outings than summer, because temperatures can swing more wildly from comfortably moderate to extremely cold, and any precipitation holds greater potential in cold temperatures to create problems for you than it does in warm temperatures. With snow and ice on the ground, the difficulty of foot travel varies more widely from fast and easy to difficult and strenuous than it does when walking on dirt and rocks in summer. In other words, there are relatively easy places and quite difficult places to go winter hiking. Don't be turned away by winter. Just choose wisely.

Fitness = Safety + Enjoyment

That equation rings true any time of year. But as with so much that we discuss in the context of winter hiking, fitness becomes more important because hiking in winter is often more strenuous than in summer and because the consequences of driving yourself to exhaustion in winter are more serious than in summer. In the backcountry, many injuries can be blamed in part on physical condition: Most accidents occur late in the day, when people are tired and more likely to fall or strain a muscle or tendon. The good news is that such injuries are largely avoidable.

Regular exercise is the key to enjoying any physical activity and minimizing the chance of injury. Maintain a program of three or four cardiovascular workouts a week of at least 30 minutes each—intense workouts that elevate your heart rate to around 80 percent of its maximum rate for your age. Try each week to also get in at least one workout (or hike) that's twice as long as your daily workouts, or longer.

It doesn't matter what form your exercise takes—walking, running, bicycling, or using aerobic machines at a health club will all keep you fit. But if you hope to head outside on snow-covered ground for full days of ski touring or snowshoeing, activities that are strenuous for the leg muscles (in large part because you're moving heavy footwear with each stride), focus some workouts on strengthening the large muscles of the legs: the quadriceps, hamstrings, and calves. Weight-lifting exercises that work those muscles, and climbing hills or stairs in a building or a stadium, all serve that end. Ultimately, the best training for an activity is that activity. If you're a snowshoer or skier, get out and snowshoe or ski, starting out slowly early in the season to avoid injuring muscles, tendons, and ligaments that have not done that specific activity in several months. Gradually increase your distance, amount of elevation gain and loss, and the weight of your pack. If you're an avid hiker through the summer and fall, it's likely your legs will be in good condition to dive into a winter of hiking, skiing, or snowshoeing.

Don't underestimate the value of 10 or 15 minutes of stretching before and after activity to slowly warm up and cool down your muscles. It reduces the chance of injury and prevents the soreness and stiffness that sometimes follow a hard hike or workout—plus it feels good. (Staying hydrated also prevents muscle stiffness and cramps; see Chapter 3.) Find stretches that isolate your major muscles, including calves, quadriceps, hamstrings, buttocks, neck, back, and shoulders. Regular abdominal exercises, such as crunches, even for a few minutes a day or a few times a week, help prevent lower-back injury provided you do them correctly.

Being in the proper condition for your activity ensures that you enjoy it more. Being exhausted and feeling your muscles cramping isn't fun. Work on staying fit year-round, and set hiking and other activity goals that are reasonable for your fitness level.

Chapter 2

Clothing and Gear

Had I sat down to write this chapter just five years ago, it would read differently than it does today. Written twenty years ago, it would sound like ancient musings found on a stone tablet on the banks of the Euphrates River. To say that outdoor gear and clothing have made huge advances in recent years only begins to tell the story. As one of *Backpacker* magazine's frequent testers of outdoor gear and technical clothing—by "technical clothing," I'm referring broadly to base, middle, and outer layers that are designed to transport moisture from your body into the air (or "breathe"), dry quickly, and in some cases trap heat efficiently relative to their weight and bulk and protect you from wind and precipitation—I'm continually amazed at the products coming out of the outdoor industry. And that's not just hyperbole.

Every year, there's new gear and clothing that excites us editors at the magazine—and we see it all, the good and the mediocre, so we're not easily excitable. The improvements are in the qualities that matter most to outdoors enthusiasts: Gear keeps getting lighter and (where appropriate) smaller while growing more functional; in short, it's just plain "smarter." Clothing keeps getting more lightweight and compact; faster drying and more breathable; and yet warmer, more weather-repellent, and more versatile—that is, individual garments increasingly more useful in a greater range of weather conditions and ensembles requiring fewer pieces and less-frequent changing of layers. The number of clothing

Winter hikers dressed for cold wind on Mount Glory in Wyoming's Teton Range

categories has even expanded—years ago, who ever heard of "soft shells"?

Clothing and gear designed for winter is a little more specialized than its three-season equivalents: Clothing is generally warmer, of course, and weather resistance becomes more important. However, there isn't an entire category of "winter clothing," per se; some three-season clothing will be functional in a winter layering system. As for the basic gear discussed in this chapter: Packs are packs—no different in summer than in winter, except that you usually need more space in winter and may want specific features; while winter footwear is an entirely different breed from the things you shod your piggies in during summertime. (Part II covers the gear and clothing needed for multi-day winter trips.) Read on.

Cool Duds for Cold Days

In clothing the constant improvement is particularly good for winter enthusiasts, for whom clothing is not only a matter of comfort but also of safety. If you're an avid three-season hiker, you've already amassed something of a technical wardrobe. That's good—you don't have to go out and spend a lot right away and may not need anything more to get started winter hiking. As you read this chapter and start spending time outdoors in temperatures well below freezing and the sometimes-cruel variety of weather that winter spits at us, you may find yourself, like many other winter warriors, adding pieces to what you already have—and being glad you did.

You know what a traditional layering system is: wind and weather shell over insulating middle layers over wicking base layers (Illustration 2-1). Base layers provide minimal insulation, transport moisture off your skin, and dry quickly. Middle layers provide most of the insulation, move moisture from inside to outside, and sometimes act as an outer layer when nothing more is needed. Shells, or outerwear, protect you from wind and precipitation while moving moisture from inside to outside. Ideally, everything layers together with a good fit that doesn't feel too bulky or restricting. Pretty basic.

However, in winter, layering becomes a much more active process than in

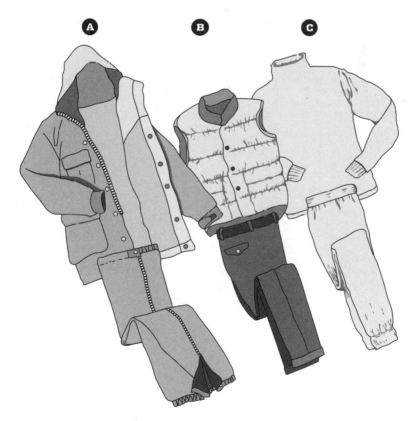

Illustration 2-1: A complete layering system for winter hiking includes, **A,** a shell jacket and pants that breathe and protect from wind and precipitation; **B,** insulating layers that trap heat, breathe well, and can be worn as an outer layer when a shell isn't needed; and, **C,** close-fitting base layers that efficiently transport moisture from the skin to the breathable outer layers.

summer—we have to be more conscious of the need to adjust layers. A slow decision to add a layer can bring on shivering within a few minutes; acting too late to remove a layer may leave you soaked with perspiration and losing precious body heat because of it. In winter, we refine our skills at layering clothing, anticipating the need for more or less based on knowing what lies ahead, rather than reacting to the situation after we've gotten too hot or too cold (see the sidebar entitled "Body Temperature Management").

The objective of a contemporary layering system is to get garments that complement one another without being overly redundant in their function—otherwise, you carry more weight and bulk and spend more money than necessary. This is true especially in winter, when you're already bringing a fair bit of duds into the backcountry with you. Understand this: Not many years ago, this point wouldn't have been raised in a discussion about layering. The different layers—base, middle, and outer—performed in specific ways. Today, garments overlap greatly in their functionality, blurring the traditional distinctions between layers, but also give us more choices and a greater ability to get exactly what each of us needs.

You can and should customize your layering system to meet your own needs. Do you get cold easily or overheat quickly on the move? Does even the slightest wind seem to slice through to bone? Do you have body parts that chill quickly— say, your hands or ears—while your head and torso always crank out heat like a nuclear reactor? How cold and wet a climate do you seek? The variety of technical wear on the market today, from base layers to shells, allows you to build an ideal layering system for your own body in winter and pick and choose garments according to the day's weather and your activity level.

Two qualities of modern technical clothing that have transformed the way we build a layering system are that (1) virtually everything is made, entirely or partly, with stretch fabrics, and (2) many fabrics have become less bulky without compromising warmth. Consequently, we can wear garments that are more close fitting without losing any freedom of movement or warmth—ideal for everything we do outdoors in winter, from hiking and snowshoeing to skiing and climbing. The reduction in bulk has tremendous advantages for day trips most of the time, but less volume of air between clothing layers somewhat reduces its performance as insulation when we're standing around in the cold. So if you expect to rest for more than a few minutes, bring a fat, warm jacket, such as a down jacket. (See Chapter 8.)

When selecting middle and outer layers for winter use—the layers that you'll take on and off during the day, depending on weather, and that will have pockets and possibly armpit zippers and other features—think about two things: (1) how easy it will be to manipulate them while wearing gloves or mittens and (2) how easy

◀ In winter, remove layers when going uphill to avoid overheating and getting wet with perspiration.

it will be to reach and manipulate their features while wearing a pack. Look for fat zipper pulls, zippers that move smoothly, and pockets and pit zips that can be reached and easily manipulated while wearing a pack. It's not a bad idea to try on a new jacket in the store while wearing mittens and a pack to get a sense of how the jacket will perform in the field.

Body Temperature Management

Earlier, I advised about getting "too hot." That suggestion might seem laughable when the thermometer reads below freezing. Nevertheless, it's actually easy to overheat when active in winter because we tend to think that we need a lot of clothing to stay warm. (Novice winter recreationists are always easy to pick out as the folks who are overdressed and sweating profusely.)

This is a critical point to emphasize. When hiking in summer we inevitably get too hot and sweat a lot, and there's not much to be done about it, but the air is generally warm enough that becoming hypothermic is not a concern. With the temperature in the thirties or lower—sometimes much lower—it's a different ball game. Getting wet leads to getting cold. Moisture on your skin and clothing conducts heat away from your body—what's called **conductive cooling**— accelerating the rate at which your body cools down. Below approximately fifty-five degrees Fahrenheit (with variation between individuals), your body can no longer produce heat fast enough to compensate for the loss of body heat through conductive cooling. Because water conducts heat much more efficiently than air does, wet clothes can bleed your body's warmth up to twenty-five times faster than if those same clothes were dry. All of the fancy clothing you're wearing has been rendered ineffective at keeping you warm because it's wet.

We all know what it feels like to get cold and wet. It's not a condition you want to suffer several miles out in the backcountry in winter. Avoid this by paying close attention to your body. When you feel yourself starting to sweat, drop a layer. Find the right selection of clothing to achieve a balance between your exertion level (how quickly you're producing body heat) and the air temperature and wind level (which are robbing your body of heat) so that you stay warm but perspire minimally or not at all. On a windless, sunny winter day with temperatures around freezing, you may actually be in shirtsleeves if you're exerting a lot, such as carrying a pack uphill. On the other hand, when you start downhill and your exertion level drops abruptly, you'll need to add clothing immediately. If it's cold at the outset of a hike, dress warmly enough that you don't spend the first half-hour shivering; but as soon as you begin to heat up, often within 10 or 20 minutes, strip off a layer. If it's snowing or raining, the ambient temperature of twenty degrees Fahrenheit or higher is usually relatively warm for winter, and many people working hard in those conditions find they don't need more than a warm shirt under a waterproof-breathable (W-B) shell to stay warm enough; wear too many layers under that shell, and you risk overheating.

Get to know your body and how it reacts to different combinations of temperature, wind, and exertion level. Anticipate the need for more or fewer layers and make the change before you start to feel cooler or warmer; then you can maintain your body in a constant, comfortable zone, avoiding the chills and sweats of winter.

Today's Technical Clothing
Base Layers

If the place where you usually recreate in winter has mild temperatures or you're one of those people who's got an internal coal-fired furnace, you may get by wearing relatively lighter long-sleeve base layers that you perhaps already own and wear on cool days and evenings in summer and fall. Most people, though, are more comfortable in warmer base layers designed for winter temperatures. They're easy to recognize in the store: The fabric is thicker than three-season jerseys, the collar is usually higher, and there's often a partial front zipper to let you ventilate.

Base layers for winter still come in a variety of thicknesses, from thin, tight-fitting long underwear tops and bottoms designed to provide fast-wicking performance beneath a warmer base layer, to so-called expedition-weight jerseys and bottoms for severe cold. Today's base layers are made with stretch fabric, allowing for a closer fit (preferred for layering close-fitting, stretchy jackets over it) without compromising range of motion. Some jerseys marry more than one type of fabric, to enhance stretch and breathability in areas such as the shoulders and sides while maximizing warmth elsewhere.

Synthetics and Wool

I know you know this stuff, so I won't bother with the old lecture about cotton. We've all discovered it doesn't work as well as synthetics, even in summer. In winter, cotton freezes quite solid. Clothing becomes a block of ice. Don't even go there. Stick with synthetics or wool. Synthetics dry quickly, breathe well, and come in many incarnations. Wool keeps you warmer when wet than synthetics, and wool and wool-synthetic blends are now more comfortable against skin (Merino wool is widely used). Yet wool dries more slowly than synthetics.

Breathable Fabrics

Ever since W.L. Gore & Associates, Inc., introduced jackets and other garments that are waterproof yet capable of releasing moisture from inside—a technological leap forward for outdoor recreation year-round but especially in winter—many in the general public seem to have concluded that all breathable garments are equally breathable. In fact, there's significant variation in just how breathable different types of fabrics and garments are. Brands evolve too quickly to evaluate here (see *Backpacker* magazine for current reviews). In general, think of breathability as a continuum that looks something like this: Anything that is waterproof is less breathable than fabrics that are not waterproof. Fabrics that are windproof and/or water-repellent (lightweight wind shells, soft shells) breathe better than waterproof fabrics but not as well as fabrics that have no wind or water resistance (basic fleece jacket). This range of breathability is something you'll notice in the field, so it's worth considering as you select garments for a layering system and your own range of activities and climate.

Insulation

The jacket, pullover, vest, and sometimes pants we wear between the base layer and shell has always been our key layer for trapping body heat, and that remains true. The difference today is that modern fabrics trap heat more efficiently, requiring less bulk than their ancestors to provide equivalent warmth. They fit more closely, thanks to stretch fabric and reduced bulk, making it easier to wear them comfortably over and under a variety of jerseys and jackets. These vests, pullovers, and jackets differ in thickness, design features (pockets, zippers, placement of stretch fabric, etc.), quality of construction, and cost. For the purposes of this discussion, I distinguish between strictly insulating layers described here and garments like soft shells and lightweight wind shells, described later, which offer wind and weather resistance. Traditional insulation such as a fleece jacket provides only warmth—it does not block wind or offer any water resistance. Insulation of this sort breathes better than anything that cuts wind or has water resistance. That makes it more desirable than a wind shell or soft shell when you just need a bit of warmth, such as on a calm winter day, or when layering it under a waterproof-breathable (W-B) shell, where any water or wind resistance is merely redundant and inhibits breathability.

Lightweight Wind Shells

These have become popular because they're compact, lightweight (for example, jackets that weigh three to eight ounces and pack down to fist size), versatile, and breathe well enough for aerobic activities (such as hiking, snowshoeing, Nordic skiing), while cutting wind and providing just enough warmth for an active person on a chilly day. Some of them keep out a light rain. They fit closely over a base layer, usually with a waistline hem and minimal pockets. You can layer an insulating fleece jacket over them, which is a reversal of the traditional layering paradigm that places the windproof layer over the insulation (though not quite as warm in wind as that traditional set-up because wind penetrates the outer fleece layer). This is a quick and smart option when there's no concern about precipitation and you need a little extra warmth. You can also usually fit a wind shell into a four-layer system consisting of base, wind shell, fleece insulation, and W-B jacket; the wind shell is redundant under a W-B jacket, but I've done just that on severely cold days when breathability was less important than warmth.

Windproof Fleece

These jackets, vests, and pants marry a windproof fabric to traditional fleece, creating a garment that both insulates and blocks wind—essentially, that combines the attributes of the two earlier categories. Thus, these are warmer than either of the earlier types of garment (although a vest obviously compromises some warmth), which is desirable when you expect a lot of wind and cold but no precipitation. You can layer a W-B jacket over windproof fleece in the event of precipitation, but

When exerting in cold temperatures, such as when cross-country skiing, a lightweight and highly breathable windproof jacket and pants provide the best balance between staying warm and overheating.

having two windproof layers inhibits breathability and makes for a warm system—which can be good or bad, depending on your needs. Windproof fleece jackets often have pit zips and mesh-lined pockets and may sport the windproof fabric only in the front, with a more breathable stretch fabric across the back (where presumably you're wearing a pack), to enhance ventilation.

Soft Shells

The term **soft shells** was born in the 1990s to refer to a new type of jacket and pant made of various fabrics that block wind, are highly water repellent (that is, they repel steady, light rain and snow), are durable and stretchy, dry fast, and breathe remarkably well for their degree of weather resistance. Within a few years after the first soft shells emerged, a profusion of them filled the market and many hailed them as the new miracle fabrics (although clothing manufacturers liked to debate the definition of "soft shell"). Indeed, these garments are highly versatile in a huge range of weather conditions, from cool to cold and dry to moderately wet conditions, making them particularly attractive to winter enthusiasts. They come in many incarnations, combinations of different types of fabric with different levels of breathability and weather resistance, and different degrees of warmth. If you don't expect to encounter much precipitation, rather than a soft shell you might better spend your money on a combination of garments from the earlier categories and a bargain W-B jacket. Soft shells are also, like W-B shells, often expensive. But a soft shell is often a better choice than a W-B shell in winter, because while it will soak through in steady rain, it easily sheds snow and is more breathable.

Waterproof-Breathable Shells

Gore-Tex has become a household word. Today, many companies in addition to W.L. Gore & Associates, Inc., make jackets and pants that use either one of the versions of Gore-Tex or their own proprietary W-B fabric. You likely own one already. These jackets and pants are windproof and waterproof and release moisture from inside, although even the best simply cannot be as breathable as garments in the earlier categories for the fact that they are designed to repel water completely. Consequently, they often have features for ventilating, such as pit zips and mesh-lined pockets that double as vents; some incorporate highly breathable stretch fabric instead of zippered vents. They usually have a durable, water-repellent coating, or **DWR,** that causes water to bead up and run off the exterior and that eventually wears off (see the sidebar entitled "Caring for Technical Clothing"). The more lightweight of these shells—some are a pound or less—are intended for three-season use but can handle moderate winter temperatures, especially if insulating layers supplement the shell. For severe winter mountain weather, you'll want a heavier (typically eighteen to twenty-five ounces), warmer, true winter shell with a fully adjustable, snug-closing hood with a bill that keeps the weather off your face.

Gloves and Mittens

Don't underestimate the importance of choosing the right gloves and/or mittens for winter hiking. Fingers and hands get cold easily and are hard to warm up again (see Chapter 4). I've always been plagued by fingertips that go numb at first exposure to anything cold and experimented for years with combinations and different models of gloves and mittens. Mittens are warmer than gloves because fingers share body heat and warm more easily when together than when isolated. However, gloves provide better dexterity, and manufacturers have reduced bulk while making gloves warmer and now use windproof fabrics. Some modular mittens with flip-open tops let you expose fingertips for brief tasks and then tuck them back inside a warm mitten. In moderate temperatures, one pair of warm gloves may be all you need. In deep cold, create a layering system that fits together without cutting off circulation, such as a liner glove as a base; an insulating glove or mitten that fits over the liner; and finally, a windproof (and ideally, W-B) shell mitten that fits over everything. A multi-layer system gives you many options for a variety of conditions.

Socks

You'll find no surprises here. In winter, you need thicker, warmer socks and often should layer a warm sock over a wicking liner sock (make sure you size boots to fit over your socks). There's a lot of good stuff out there. Wool (Merino, again) is a top performer, along with synthetics. Makers of quality socks are building in extra padding and elasticity where needed. Today's socks for outdoor recreation can be worn for multiple days (depending on how wet you get them). They cost more, but this is an area where your money is well spent.

Head Wear

As with gloves, head wear is something that's important to customize to your personal needs. In winter, I use five different types of head wear, choosing them depending on my activity and the length of time I'll be out, and sometimes carry as many as three of them with me. Here is the system I've developed for myself:
1. An earband made of windproof fabric for when I'm working hard in moderate temperatures but need to keep my ears warm (and to some extent, keep sweat out of my eyes)
2. A lightweight wool or synthetic hat for aerobic activity on a cold day
3. A thick, warmer hat for a moderate activity level on a cold day or for rest breaks
4. A lightweight synthetic **balaclava** for moderate activity level on a very cold day
5. An expedition-weight, fleece-lined balaclava for severe cold (or for the campsite; see Chapter 8)

Whatever you choose, remember that your head releases a lot of heat—give yourself enough head wear options to release that heat to avoid overheating and to contain it when you need the warmth. Carrying extra head wear is wise (especially in an emergency), given the amount of warmth gained per square foot of fabric you carry.

Gaiters

Gaiters wrap around the lower legs from the boot uppers to just below the knee, closing in front with a zipper or **hook-and-loop** strips (for example, Velcro). A strap wraps from the gaiter bottom under the arch of your boot, and often a small hook grabs the laces to hold the gaiter onto the boot. Gaiters keep snow out, which is critical when snowshoeing or ski touring in powder or wet snow. They should be water-resistant at a minimum, preferably waterproof, and breathable—though you obviously pay more for W-B. They also provide a surprising amount of warmth for your lower legs and feet, which can be the coldest part of your body. Their warmth makes them desirable on a cold day and undesirable on a relatively mild day, when you'll want to release that heat to keep your feet from sweating too much. Low gaiters, which extend from boot uppers to around the bottom of the

Caring for Technical Clothing

There's no doubt about it: This stuff costs some dough. Although it's worth every buck when your butt's out in freezing temperatures, you want to make your technical clothing last as long as possible. Here are some ways to do that:

▲ Dirt deteriorates fabrics and can take the durable, water-repellent coating, or DWR, off W-B and water-resistant garments. Follow washing instructions on the garment label or check the manufacturer's recommendations (often available at the company's website).

▲ Most garments should be washed in warm or cold water, gentle cycle; a few manufacturers recommend dry cleaning. Some suggest using only front-loading washers without an agitator and nondetergent cleaners such as Nikwax Tech Wash or McNett X-Treme Wash for technical garments.

▲ Synthetic base layers can withstand many days of use without washing and still move moisture off your skin. However, the perspiration salts that accumulate in the fabric are a desiccant (that is, they absorb moisture) and will dry and irritate your skin if not laundered. Skin moisturizer addresses the problem on an extended trip.

▲ Many synthetics (including most base layers and soft shells) and Merino wool are degraded by dryer heat. Hang them to dry indoors (UV rays also break down synthetics, although slowly).

▲ Wash your W-B jacket when it's dirty—perhaps twice a year. It breathes and repels moisture better when clean. Dirt works into the interstitial spaces in fabric and literally cuts through the yarns as it is worked back and forth, which can give the jacket a fuzzy look and wear off its DWR. The DWR is also compromised by campfire smoke and skin oils, eventually causing the jacket to "wet out" or appear to absorb water; it isn't actually, but once wet it conducts heat away from your body, so you'll feel colder. Wash the jacket only when necessary—laundering will wear the DWR off but only after twenty or more washings.

▲ Manufacturers differ on whether to put a garment with a membrane in the dryer: Some say dryer heat restores the DWR; others warn that dryer heat can cook the membrane and advise hanging the jacket to dry. Check the manufacturer's recommendations; when in doubt, hang dry it.

▲ Check the manufacturer's recommendations on washing a W-B jacket. Some advise using a nondetergent soap like Nikwax Tech Wash; others recommend a small amount of powder laundry detergent. Dryer heat often reactivates the DWR, but some garments should be dried on low heat.

▲ If washing and drying fails to restore the DWR, try reapplying the DWR using any of several products on the market, such as Nikwax TX Direct or Gore's Revivex (check the manufacturer's recommendation).

▲ A technical garment is dead when you see layers delaminating, seams coming apart, or similar irreversible damage.

▲ Wash a down-insulated garment only when absolutely necessary, and always use a mild, down soap only. Detergents strip down feathers of their protective oils. Drying a down jacket (or sleeping bag) is tricky and not always successful—the down may clump or tear, thus damaging the product.

▲ Anything made of nylon will melt if brought too close to a flame.

calf, are a good option for balancing the need to keep snow out of your boots with the need to avoid overheating.

Sunglasses and Goggles

Protecting your eyes from bright sunlight and ultraviolet (UV) rays becomes more important when the ground is covered with snow—which reflects most of the sunlight striking it—especially at higher elevations. Sunglasses should wrap around the eyes for full coverage, or, as with glacier goggles, provide fabric shields at the corners of the eyes. Get tinted lenses to minimize the amount of light reaching your eyes—twenty percent tinting for most outdoor activities (but only five to ten percent for mountaineering). Polarized lenses reduce glare. Yellow lenses improve visibility on foggy or gray days. Put a keeper cord on your sunglasses so they don't blow or fall off. For an all-day outing on a bright day, bring a spare pair of shades, preferably in a hard case so they don't get crushed in your pack. Goggles, such as the kind alpine skiers wear, are only necessary when you're in severe cold and strong wind—with windchills well below zero degrees Fahrenheit—where you must cover up every inch of flesh, including your eyes, which can be damaged by the cold or flying ice particles and can literally freeze shut.

Face Mask

As with goggles, you'll only need a face mask on the coldest of nasty, cold days, in a strong wind—in fact, the wind is the biggest concern because it can freeze exposed flesh, causing frostbite. Your nose and cheeks are vulnerable in cold that severe. Most people simply avoid going outside when it's that cold. If you don't shy away from those conditions, get a simple face mask made of neoprene or a similar material that won't ice up when the condensation from your breath collects on it. If your nose or face stings badly from the cold wind, you'll know it's time to put on the mask.

Most manufacturers will repair or replace garments that fail before their expected life span. Contact the company's customer service department. This stuff is made tough, but being a little careful with it when in the backcountry can't hurt.

Winter Boots
Buying Smart

As with footwear for three-season hiking, the most important factor in choosing boots for winter is the fit. If pulling up lame with blisters or severe discomfort is an inconvenience in summertime, it can pose a serious danger if you're way out there in winter. You may read a great review or hear a glowing recommendation about a particular model, but if the shoe doesn't fit, don't wear it. Manufacturers all use their own **lasts** in making boots—the last essentially being the model "foot" around which their boots are constructed—and the key to good performance and comfort is finding a manufacturer that makes boots that make your feet smile. Most boot makers now carry men's and women's models in winter boots, so women don't have to settle for boots that are too wide. Only by trying on many models and walking around the store in them can you judge which fits you best.

The following are some tips on fitting your boots:

▲ Always buy shoes later in the day, because your feet swell during the day.

▲ Try on boots while wearing your hiking socks.

▲ Look for wiggle room for your toes. Have about a thumbs' width of space between your big and second toes and the end of the shoe; toes should not slam against the front of the boot when walking downhill.

▲ Your foot should not slide forward or backward in the boot, and your heel shouldn't move more than a quarter-inch when you walk.

▲ Make sure the boot's cuff doesn't contact your ankle or shin uncomfortably when walking with the boots laced.

▲ With the laces tied, you should have range in the lacing to loosen or tighten them up further. (On the trail, you may want to tighten laces to stabilize your foot inside the boot going downhill or loosen them going uphill when your foot needs to flex more.)

Wear new boots at home or around town before your first hike in them—some may require breaking-in, but at a minimum you should make sure the fit is right before wearing them for hours on a hike and give your feet a chance to get used to them.

Unlike three-season footwear, the other important qualities to look for in winter boots are warmth and weather resistance. You gotta keep them piggies warm and dry so that you'll have them along on all future hikes. Unless you never expect to get your boots wet, go for waterproof boots. Breathable boots reduce how much your feet sweat. Those two qualities are generally achieved through the incorporation of a W-B liner (such as Gore-Tex) in the boot, which also tends to make the boot a little warmer—a positive thing in winter.

Modern boots for winter hiking and snowshoeing (you can use the same boots for both activities) and ski touring (which requires specialized boots; see later) are less bulky and clumsy than ten or twenty years ago but toasty warm thanks to insulation that's less bulky. Uppers made of synthetics and W-B membranes replacing heavier materials like leather, suede, and rubber have made boots lighter—which translates to you walking farther with less fatigue.

When shopping for boots, consider the temperatures and amount of snow you'll typically encounter. Some manufacturers give winter boots a temperature rating that supposedly represents the lowest temperature at which they'll be comfortable, but consider the rating just a rough guideline and if you care about ratings, select boots rated as much as twenty degrees lower than the coldest temperature you anticipate actually seeing. More important than any rating is that the boots are well insulated; have a thick sole for insulation against the frozen ground; provide good support under the heel and arch and around the ankle; have a tread that provides good traction on frozen ground, snow, and ice; and appear durable, with features like a thick toe rand, or bumper.

If your winter hiking destinations typically receive little or no snow, a mid-cut boot that comes up to around your ankle will serve you well. In the unusual event of snow, you can always wear gaiters over the boots. If you get out in a lot of snow, the decision between mid-cut and high-cut may come down to whether you want the extra warmth and support gained by the higher boot. With a mid-cut boot, you still have the option of using gaiters and probably will be wearing them anyway in snow. Some winter boot models come with built-in gaiters that can be rolled up. They may offer a price advantage over buying boots and gaiters separately and some convenience in the field, but make sure the gaiter doesn't get in the way or trap body heat when not in use.

If you're looking for boots to use with snowshoes, put the boots and snowshoes on together in the store. Make sure the former fits in the latter's binding (rarely a problem, unless you have an unusually wide boot or the snowshoe binding interferes with the boot lacing or a buckle) and that you like how they feel together.

I'm only going to touch on the use of crampons with boots. Be aware that only certain boots accept crampons, and the type of crampon-compatible boot you'd select depends on the type of crampons you want to put on the boots; furthermore, the type of crampons you select depends on the sort of mountain climbing you plan to do. That's intentionally vague because this book is not a guide to technical climbing; there are good books available that cover the subject well (see Appendix B). Do some research before purchasing crampons and boots for them.

In boots for ski touring, you still want warmth, water resistance, breathability, and support, but you also need good flexibility because you're constantly flexing your ankle and foot forward and backward. Traditionally, these boots were made of leather, but more and more boots substitute synthetic materials in the uppers for leather. Touring boots come up to the ankle or above it. Some have a plastic cuff or ankle strap for added support.

Taking Care of Your Boots

Boots for winter hiking or snowshoeing are big, tough boots. They should last you many years of moderate use, and if they don't, contact the manufacturer to get them replaced. Still, they'll suffer some abuse through normal use, and proper care can extend their life span. Keep these tips in mind:

▲ Use a stiff brush and water to clean off excessive dirt, mud, or road salt.

▲ Dry boots out thoroughly after each hike. Always remove the insole to let it dry. Stuff balled-up newspaper into each boot for a few hours to absorb moisture and prevent the build-up of smelly, damaging mildew. Don't leave boots for a prolonged period in a cold place (like your car trunk) where they won't dry out.

▲ Don't dry boots in the sun or near a heat source.

▲ Store boots in a warm, dry place out of direct sunlight.

▲ Periodically spray inside your boots with an antibacterial foot or shoe spray.

▲ If the boots have a W-B liner, occasionally clean it by swishing a little clean water inside the boots.

With leather boots, at the beginning and end of each hiking season—or more often if you use them frequently—treat the leather with a waterproofing product to help it continue to shed water and keep it from drying out.

A Pack for Winter

Yes, that phrase "a pack for winter" is a tad misleading. No, you don't need a special pack for winter hiking. You may already own a pack that's ideal for winter day trips. However, the additional clothing and gear that winter demands we carry, especially on longer hikes, and the specialized gear required for some outings may lead you to the revelation that your summer day pack doesn't have the capacity or design features for your winter outings. (I'm slightly embarrassed to confess that I own several packs, but only two or three of them do what I ask of a pack in winter.) Pack makers are increasingly designing technical day packs for activities such as backcountry skiing and snowboarding, climbing, and winter hiking that simply have a little more capacity and activity-specific features than you'll find on basic, less-expensive day packs.

If you already own a pack that seems adequate for your winter hikes, use it. Experience, your type of activity, how much you carry, and the degree of organization you like in a pack will, in time, help refine your sense of what you want in a pack for winter. Wait until you have a better idea of that before sinking money into another pack. If the pack you already use in the other three seasons is clearly inadequate for winter hiking, the following advice will help you select a new one.

Whatever season is its intended use, a pack should perform two functions well:

1. Fit what you need to carry
2. Feel comfortable from the moment you put it on until you take it off

Some people, especially those who haven't carried many different packs, don't place enough importance in the second criterion. That's simply because the external design and features of a pack are its most obvious qualities, and differences in the

A winter day-trip pack should have enough capacity for all your gear, clothing, food, and water and should include external attachments or compression straps for holding things such as snowshoes.

suspension system—the hipbelt, shoulder straps, and the internal frame (back pad, stays, and/or frame sheet)—don't usually leap out at you visually. Yet the suspension (that is, *comfort*) is more important, because it will dictate how the pack carries. The suspension's comfort and precision fit is what you're paying for when you buy a high-end pack. Shop first for comfort, then for features.

The two functions listed earlier are certainly generalizations. What you need to fit inside the pack depends not only on your chosen activity but also on where you're going and for how long, the weather, and other factors that can vary from one trip to the next. (See "Traveling Light Vs. Safety.") How much you value a pack's degree of organization—pockets that provide quick access to items and external features for attaching gear—comes down as much to personal preference as anything. Those features also affect a pack's weight and shape, both of which may be important to you. How comfortably the pack carries depends on variables such as how much you're willing to spend, how important minimizing weight is to you (for example, a beefier, more comfortable suspension weighs more), and whether you're loading more weight into a pack than it's intended to carry.

The next section outlines qualities to consider when selecting a pack for winter, in the order I think will help you quickly narrow the list of candidates—that is, you should eliminate first any packs that aren't the right capacity, then those that don't meet your standard for comfort, and so on. You may decide to give more or less weight to each depending on your own needs and wants. Virtually all day packs in the capacity range used by most winter day-trippers are internal frame (see Chapter 8).

Capacity

For a short hike or aerobic skiing or snowshoeing workout when the weather or getting stranded for hours without help are not issues, you don't need more than a small hydration pack, day pack, or lumbar pack (the same one you'd use in summer). However, for an outing of a few hours or more, especially anywhere you could encounter severe weather or will venture more than an hour from the nearest road, you'll need a pack in the range of 1500 cubic inches to just more than 3000 cubic inches, or roughly 24 to 50 liters. Packs at the lower end of that broad range will fit one person's clothing, water, and food for a day trip, plus a little emergency gear (first-aid kit, small sleeping bag, bivy bag). At the upper end of that range, you'll fit more emergency gear (winter bag, stove and fuel, etc.), plus any specialized gear you may need for, say, climbing a mountain or backcountry skiing.

Comfort

In winter, warm clothing provides padding, so you don't need as much of it in a pack's hipbelt and shoulder straps as in summer. A thin nylon belt and relatively thin shoulder straps are adequately comfortable and have the added benefit of being less obtrusive and helping to reduce the pack's weight. Still, there's great variation in the degree of comfort offered by different packs' suspension systems—and in how adjustable they are for finding a precise fit—and variation in the dimensions of human torsos. Look also at a pack's load control: how well it clings to your back and keeps the pack from shifting as you move, which becomes more important when you're on skis or snowshoes or hiking on slippery ground. A pack's suspension system, shape, how it's loaded, and how well it compresses and stabilizes a load when not completely full all affect load control. Consider how much weight you'll carry: You'll need only a simple suspension (a nylon webbing belt, thin shoulder straps, a thin back pad doubling as a "frame") to carry ten pounds but may want a little more to the pack (some padding in the shoulder straps and perhaps in the belt, perhaps a frame sheet or frame stays and/or a little more padding for your back) if you're carrying twenty or twenty-five pounds. Check out several packs before choosing; only you can decide how important comfort is to you (see "Fitting a Pack").

Access and Features

Although capacity matters, the access and features a pack has greatly affect the functionality of the pack's space. If minimizing pack weight is your highest priority, get a simple top-loading rucksack with no more external features than you want; some basic packs, for instance, don't even have a lid pocket. External lid, side, or back pockets let you organize things and provide quick access to items; but think about whether you want to attach gear (for example, skis) to your pack and how external pockets could get in the way. One handy feature for numerous functions is a shovel, or shove-it, pocket on the back side of the pack, which provides a quick and sometimes voluminous stash for things such as a jacket, food, and wet items. A side zipper that accesses the main compartment is another way to get quick access to a jacket or food, but it doesn't add the bulk of side pockets. An ice ax loop or two are often standard features, but it's more convenient when the upper attachment strap for an ax has a quick-release buckle. Similarly, some packs have loops and/or quick-release straps for trekking poles. Side compression straps should work well enough to stabilize the pack's contents when it's not entirely full, to prevent contents from shifting. Quick-release buckles on side compression straps make attaching or removing skis, poles, or **wands** easier, especially with gloved hands. (You may have to carry skis or snowshoes on your pack if lower-elevation trails are snow-free but snow will be found at higher elevations.)

Water Access

At any time of year, I give high priority to having access to water without having to remove my pack. In a day pack, the most efficient design is a so-called **hydration system** (one of those ingeniously vague marketing terms that sounds high tech), consisting of a hose with a mouthpiece running from a water bladder inside the pack to the shoulder straps, giving you instant access to water without having to stop. A hydration system does not affect the pack's shape—unlike sticking bottles in side pockets, which makes your pack wider—and a bladder won't fall out of your pack the way a bottle can tumble out of an exterior pocket (which seems to happen more in winter, when you're doing things like clambering over blow downs in snowshoes or skis). The better bladder-hose systems now have turn-off valves on the mouthpiece to prevent dripping. For freezing temperatures, look for a hose that's insulated to prevent it from freezing. (The bladder is close enough to your body that it won't freeze unless you hit really cold temperatures.) The alternative to a hydration system is bottle pockets on the side of the pack, or a pocket or similar small accessory that attaches to your shoulder straps or elsewhere on the pack (often purchased separately). Bottle pockets are also handy places to stash gloves and other small items, but make sure you can easily reach them when wearing the pack—I've seen a surprising number of packs with bottle pockets that are difficult or impossible to reach while wearing the pack—and consider whether the pockets will get in the way of attaching anything to the pack (such as skis).

Weight

It doesn't make sense to get any piece of gear that's heavier than it needs to be. The largest technical packs for winter day trips need not weigh more than three or four pounds when empty, and the lightest in the range described earlier will weigh about a pound. The trade-offs for reduced weight are less suspension system and fewer features. In short, go as light as possible, but don't sacrifice a comfort level or features that are important to you merely to shave ounces.

Durability

As long as you buy a pack intended for backcountry use—as opposed to a book or travel pack—it's likely to last. Winter doesn't inherently put more wear on a pack than summer; actually, contact with snow is much easier on any gear than rock or dirt. Avoid budget packs from brands that you don't recognize as a respected maker of outdoor gear.

Fitting a Pack

If a pack does not carry comfortably, it's either not fitted properly or is not the right size for your torso; knowing how to fit a pack is critical to your comfort when carrying it. Many day packs cannot be adjusted for different torso lengths (discussed later) but will fit a limited range of torsos and come in at least two sizes of suspension system (hipbelt, shoulder straps, and connected parts). Some come in women's models designed for their shorter torsos and wider hips.

The guidelines for fitting a pack don't differ with the season. Start by measuring your torso: Stand at attention and have someone extend a soft tape measure from your seventh vertebra—the prominent bone at the base of your neck—along your spine to the top of your hipbones, which you can find by placing your hands on your hips and drawing a line between your thumbs. If you don't have a cloth tape measure, use a string and then hold the measured string to a yardstick. A knowledgeable gear retailer will be able to find packs that fit your torso.

Try on many packs, wearing the type of clothing you'd wear when winter hiking and loading the pack with what you'll carry in the backcountry. Loosen the suspension straps. Buckle the belt and chest strap. With the hipbelt resting atop your hipbones—not sliding down over them—pull the belt comfortably snug. Tighten the stabilizer straps, beginning with the lowest if there's more than one. Next, tighten the load-lifters, which should lie at an angle forty-five degrees to your shoulders. Finally, tighten the shoulder straps and chest strap as desired.

You should have leeway in the belt and all straps to loosen or tighten further. The shoulder straps should wrap cleanly around your shoulders, without gaps or bunching, and extend about a hand's width beneath your armpits.

When properly adjusted, about two-thirds of the pack's weight should ride on your hips, the rest on your shoulders and upper back.

Walk around the store wearing your loaded pack. If it doesn't feel comfortable, find another one.

On the trail, make slight adjustments for comfort in varied terrain. For instance, loosening the hipbelt and stabilizer straps slightly gives your hips and legs extra mobility for going uphill. Tightening everything stabilizes your load to prevent it throwing you off-balance going downhill.

Pack Care

A good pack made by a respected manufacturer will probably last through many years of hard use, and if it doesn't, contact the manufacturer via its customer service phone number or its website and ask them to repair the pack. Most will do it free, although they'll ask you to cover the cost of shipping the pack. Still, taking care of a pack can extend its life a few years. Clean it out after every trip. Open all pockets and compartments and shake out crumbs, dirt, and sand. Never leave wet things, like clothing, inside a pack; dampness promotes the growth of mildew, which can deteriorate any fabric, including nylon. If the pack is dirty, sponge it off with mild soap and water. Hang it to dry out of the sun; UV rays damage nylon. Inspect your pack for loose seams or deteriorating hardware at major stress points around the hipbelt, shoulder straps, and other load-bearing points: Better to detect a strap, zipper, or buckle that's about to blow before your hike rather than having to deal with it deep in the woods, especially on a cold day. Store your pack in a cool, dry, airy place out of direct sunlight.

Loading a Pack

Sure, you can just throw everything inside your pack. But as you've probably already discovered on your three-season hikes, how you load a pack makes a big difference in how well it carries. Loading your pack in an organized way also helps you locate things quickly—and you don't want to fumble around looking for a warm jacket or hat when the temperature's far below freezing and the wind's howling (Illustration 2-2). Keep these tips in mind:

▲ Keep things to which you want instant access (map, compass, light source, batteries, first-aid kit, jacket) in an accessory pocket or near the top of the main compartment. Items needed only on a rest stop can go deeper inside the main compartment (lunch, extra water, and clothing).

▲ If your pack is minimalist and lacks pockets, place small items together in a stuff sack to avoid losing them amid everything else. If the pack has a key lanyard, clip the stuff sack to it.

▲ On a good trail, if you're carrying more than ten or fifteen pounds, load most

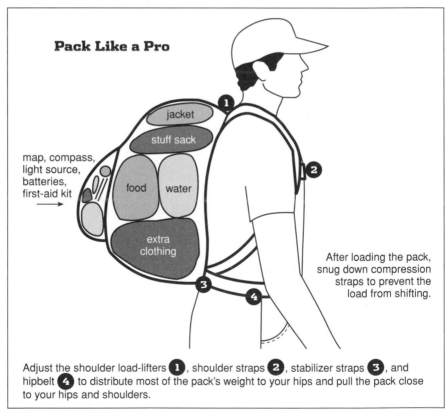

Pack Like a Pro

jacket

stuff sack

map, compass, light source, batteries, first-aid kit →

food   water

extra clothing

After loading the pack, snug down compression straps to prevent the load from shifting.

Adjust the shoulder load-lifters **1** , shoulder straps **2** , stabilizer straps **3** , and hipbelt **4** to distribute most of the pack's weight to your hips and pull the pack close to your hips and shoulders.

Illustration 2-2: An organized and properly loaded pack fits comfortably and allows you to find things quickly.

of the weight high in the pack, close to your shoulders, and place lighter items at the bottom. Women whose legs are long relative to their torso may prefer centering the weight slightly lower. If there are any hard or sharp objects that could poke you in the back, use soft items, like a fleece jacket, to pad them. Once the pack is loaded, tighten all compression straps to prevent any shifting of the contents, which could throw you off-balance on the trail.

▲ For hilly ski touring or a trail where you'll have to clamber over many blow downs, you may want to keep the weight a little lower in the pack—and make sure no straps or gear on the pack's exterior can snag on branches or other natural snaggers. If necessary, loosen the load-lifters slightly for greater range of arm motion. Tighten the sternum strap to compensate. The shoulder straps should be tight enough to prevent the load from shifting and help "tow" the packbag through thick vegetation.

Poles

Trekking or ski poles may or may not be something you already use for three-season hiking. If you do use them, you know they greatly reduce the strain on leg muscles and joints, especially knees—and if you don't use them in summer but you have knee, foot, ankle, back, or other problems, you should be using poles.

In winter, poles are virtually mandatory gear. When you're on snow, whether snowshoeing, skiing, or hiking in boots or crampons, poles aid with balance (remember, falls are more likely on this slippery surface, and the consequences of injury are more serious) and relieve your back and leg muscles and joints of some of the strain of an activity that's usually more strenuous in winter than summer. Even on dry ground, you're often carrying more weight in winter, and you can encounter icy or wet spots where you'll appreciate the assistance of poles. And forget about picking up a stout walking stick on the trail: It may be buried under snow or frozen into the ground, it won't hold any weight without sinking into snow, and it's much colder than the cork or rubber handles of poles.

Fixed-length poles for traditional ski touring are certainly adequate, provided they're the right length for you (coming to shoulder height when stood upright at your side). However, adjustable poles are ideal—that is, telescoping poles with two or three sections. You can lengthen or shorten them for the steepness of a slope when going uphill or downhill. When collapsed and tucked under a pack's compression straps, they protrude little, if at all. The design of pole hand straps keeps improving in terms of comfort, how securely they stay on, and how well they prevent your hands from fatigue and blisters (the latter especially when not wearing gloves). The baskets are removable, so you can use the poles without baskets for three-season hiking, then install wide snow baskets for winter. Some poles have built-in springs for shock absorption. If you intend to venture where avalanches loom as a potential hazard, some poles convert quickly into an avalanche probe (see "Other Gear").

Ski poles—preferably adjustable—are essential when hiking on snow, snowshoeing, or skiing to aid balance and relieve the legs and lower back of some of the physical stress.

Ice Ax and Crampons

You may never hike anyplace where you'll need an ice ax and crampons—but don't assume you won't. Although these tools may seem to the winter novice like weapons for battle used only by mountaineers, they are standard gear in many places where, even on trail, you'll have to ascend, descend, or cross snow-covered slopes.

Where do you need an ax and crampons? Basically, anyplace where there exists the potential for falling and sliding far enough on snow or ice that you could get hurt. That includes open snow slopes in meadows or above tree line and steep hiking trails—even in heavily wooded areas—in wet mountain climates where long tongues of ice can often fill the entire trail. If it looks like you could slide a long way, odds are you could, and therefore you should carry an ax and probably wear crampons. However, even relatively low-angle slopes can present a danger of falling, given the slickness of nylon and other technical clothing often worn in snow. The more firm the snow's surface—as opposed to deep powder that you sink into—the easier it is to slide out of control.

When the ground is covered with ice or firmly frozen snow, wear crampons for safety, to enhance traction, and to move more quickly with less effort. ▶

An important safety note: Possessing a mountaineering ax and crampons does not by itself prepare you for safely negotiating an open, potentially dangerous snow slope. Without the knowledge of how to use them, especially the ax to **self-arrest,** you don't belong out there and should find safer terrain that's more appropriate to your skills and experience. As mentioned earlier, this book is not intended as a guide to technical climbing, but it's important that you realize the potential hazards of falling and sliding and understand that you'll need an ax and crampons in some places. The advice given here about using these things should not, however, be considered more than a basic tutorial. Before hiking anyplace where you'll need crampons and especially an ax, read more and have someone knowledgeable about their use give you a live demonstration on snow of how to walk on crampons and self-arrest with an ax.

An ice ax consists of a shaft (traditionally wooden, now more often a lightweight, tough metal such as aluminum or titanium), a pointed spike at the bottom end, and a head with a *pick* (the pointed end) and *adze* (the broad end). For winter hiking or general mountaineering, your correct ax length is determined by holding the ax loosely in your cupped fingers, with you arm straight down at your side: The spike should come to your ankle. (Much shorter axes are used for steeper, technical ice climbing and mountaineering.)

On a steep slope, an ice ax can double as a trekking pole for balance or to help haul yourself up through trees or dense vegetation. Its most important function, however, is as a safety tool, both to help prevent a slide and to stop yourself, or self-arrest, if you do fall and slide. When crossing, ascending, or descending a slope of concern, carry the ax in your uphill hand, in a grip that prepares you for an emergency self-arrest: with the adze facing forward, the thumb under the adze, and the fingers and palm wrapped around the pick near the shaft. Plant the ax firmly in the snow with each step up. If you slip and fall, drive the shaft into the snow as an anchor and hold on tightly. If this fails and you slide, self-arrest by holding the ax across your chest with one hand on the head and the other low on the shaft, with the pick facing away from your body; roll toward the head of the ax (rather than the spike, or bottom of the shaft), and plant the pick into the snow as a brake. This must be done immediately, or you may soon be sliding too quickly and uncontrollably to effectively self-arrest.

Crampons alone can be useful on trails that are prone to getting icy, as in wet climates like the Northeast and Pacific Northwest. Crampons vary from climbing models with twelve "points," or metal teeth, to simpler versions with just four or six points that strap onto a boot and provide traction on ice—the latter intended for icy trails where a long fall is not a concern and you don't need an ax and full crampons. The trail need not be steep or pose the potential for a long, sliding fall to be slippery enough that you'd want crampons to keep yourself from tumbling and fracturing a wrist or elbow. Basic strap-on, ten-point, or twelve-point crampons are more than adequate on an icy trail and will function well on easier mountaineering routes up peaks. Unlike more technical crampons for ice climbing or serious mountaineering, strap-on crampons do not require stiff boots; many strap-on models will fit on standard, flexible, lightweight hiking boots. Make sure the crampons fit on your boots before trying them on a real hike; you'll usually have to adjust the crampon length once to fit your boots, a task more easily done in the warmth of your home than on the trail.

Know also when you shouldn't use crampons: When snow is so wet that it's balling, or clumping up into round balls, and sticking to the bottom of your crampons, remove the crampons and walk in your boots. Balling snow in crampons can easily cause you to fall.

All those sharp points make an ax and crampons the most dangerous gear you're likely to carry. When they're on your pack, cover those points with rubber guards, which are inexpensive and widely available at retailers of mountain gear.

Snowshoes

If you're new to hitting trails in winter, snowshoes are your most likely first choice as a mode of transportation. They are much more intuitive to use than skis, and most people lacking any experience with either snowshoes or skis feel more comfortable using snowshoes, especially on hills—to put it bluntly, you'll fall down less. When it comes to getting up and down steep, narrow trails, skiing is out of the question for all but the most expert skiers, while beginners can snowshoe virtually anything their first time out.

The technology behind snowshoes has improved dramatically in recent years: Bindings are easier to operate yet more secure, frames have gotten lighter and more streamlined yet stronger, and cutting-edge materials are used in everything from the frame to the decking. On a fundamental level, snowshoes haven't changed since humans first noticed that hares and other wide-footed animals moved over snow well: They still consist of a wide platform, usually some kind of decking material stretched across a frame (although sometimes a solid piece of molded plastic), with a binding that secures your boot. Although some manufacturers crank out snowshoes with wood frames and rawhide decking, the vast majority of today's models are made of modern, lightweight, and durable materials, simply because they work.

Shop around and you'll notice significant variation in the prices of snowshoe models, although differently priced models may look similar, from the bindings to the frame and decking materials. Deciding how much to spend essentially boils down to one question: How hard will you use them? Increasing price in snowshoes correlates closely with better durability for hard, frequent use. The more expensive models are built to specifications to sustain harder use.

Before buying, consider these things about where you'll usually wear the snowshoes:

▲ The steepness of the terrain
▲ How far you'll usually hike

- How much weight you'll carry
- How much you'll use the snowshoes
- How far into the backcountry you intend to walk and the consequences of breaking a binding or other snowshoe part way out there

More affordable models (sometimes called "recreational" or "hiking" snowshoes) are designed for occasional outings on flat ground and gentle hills where the snow is often packed or not deep. They'll last for many years of moderate use, but they're not made for frequent forays into the mountains for long days.

Stepping up in price you get into what may be called "rugged hiking" snowshoes. Their bindings, frame, decking, and other parts—especially the construction, all the connections and places where the snowshoe might break under stress—are built to handle many long days on steep trails. These snowshoes may have noticeable enhancements like larger teeth on the cleats or may be heavier than recreational snowshoes.

A third category more clearly defined than the previous two consists of racing, or trail running, snowshoes. These look different than the types described earlier: short and narrow, with sharply tapered or asymmetrical tails. The bindings hold your feet securely. They are about two-thirds the weight of snowshoes in the earlier categories. They won't float as well in deep powder, but that's not their intended use. These snowshoes offer maximum agility for the niche sport of running or racing on trails covered with packed (usually groomed) snow. The least expensive of these models compare in price with the most-expensive rugged hiking snowshoes, and you'll pay a premium for models made of durable, super light materials like titanium cleats and a carbon fiber frame.

Lastly, several manufacturers produce snowshoes for children weighing up to eighty or ninety pounds (including their packs). Children's models measure roughly 7 by 18 inches, are typically made of aluminum or plastic, and have features comparable with recreational adult snowshoes, although they cost much less. They are durable for easy outings, but most are not built for hard backcountry use. If your child wants to head into the mountains with you, think about outfitting him or her in a pair of small men's or women's snowshoes.

Sizing Up Your Snowshoes

After determining the type of snowshoe you need, you need to know your size and how to evaluate in the store how well a snowshoe will perform in the backcountry. Here are a few tips.

Your snowshoe size is dictated by your total weight, including body, pack, boots, and clothing. Check the manufacturer's recommended weight range for

◀ When traveling in deep snow, snowshoes keep you from postholing (sinking in to your thighs or crotch), provide traction, and allow you to go up and down steep terrain.

each size snowshoe they produce. Women's snowshoes come in different sizes than men's. As a rough guideline, figure that in wet, heavy snow, 8-inch-by-22-inch snowshoes carry up to 150 pounds, 8-inch-by-25-inch up to 200 pounds, 9-inch-by-34-inch up to 250 pounds, and 9.5-inch-by-36-inch up to 300 pounds. For deep powder, step up one snowshoe size for each weight category.

The smaller the snowshoe, the more agile it is for clambering over blow downs and through brush. The larger the snowshoe, the better the flotation atop snow. If you're in between weight categories, get the smaller snowshoe if you typically encounter heavy snow and the larger size if you're getting into deep backcountry powder.

The weight of your snowshoes matters: A pound on your feet is equal to 6.4 pounds on your back, so heavier snowshoes will fatigue you more quickly than lightweight snowshoes. However, don't sacrifice the performance or durability you need to save a bit on weight.

Although all of the major components of a snowshoe (listed later) are important, the binding may affect your satisfaction with the snowshoe more than anything else may. Most manufacturers have kept pace with the technological advances of recent years, but still, bindings vary significantly in design, security, and durability, both between snowshoes in different categories and between models in the same categories. Any binding should hold your boot securely, preventing your heel from sliding to either side, even when sidehilling across a slope. In any category of snowshoe, you want a binding made of hardy, flexible rubberized or nylon straps, with buckles that don't loosen or freeze and are easily manipulated even in mittens. Most bindings fit a wide range of men's and women's boot sizes.

The binding pivots on either a thick rubber strap or a rod below the ball of your foot. These come in two types: the perhaps more-popular fixed rotation, which lifts the snowshoe tail up with your foot, and free rotation, which does not lift the tail. Fixed-rotation bindings throw snow onto your back and butt but are more agile when you have to climb over forest obstacles. Free-rotation bindings won't hurl snow onto your back, but the droopy tails may get hung up in vegetation or downed trees. Think about the trails where you'll snowshoe in considering which you'd prefer.

The cleats beneath your toes and heel are what provide you with traction, and big teeth mean better grip on snow or ice. Most cleats are made of aluminum or stainless steel; the former is lighter, but ices up more easily. Look for a de-icing pad beneath the toe cleat to keep snow from clumping up in solid, frozen baseballs underfoot (which can send you sliding and tumbling). Lastly, look for teeth along the frame sides for lateral traction, especially important for traversing a slope.

You may still find someone making traditional snowshoes with a wooden frame and rawhide decking, but most snowshoes are made of more durable modern materials: lightweight aluminum frames and a decking made of either rubberlike hypalon (which grips snow best and is tough), solid plastic (which relies on an underside pattern for traction), or polyurethane-coated nylon (slippery but durable).

The best way to find the right snowshoes is to rent various models before buying. That will let you evaluate whether you like the binding's operation and security, how well the cleat grips snow, fixed-rotation vs. free-rotation models, the snowshoe size (if you're on the borderline for weight), and even the snowshoes' shape and width.

Skis

Skis are the equipment of choice for many winter enthusiasts when the terrain is flat to gently rolling, or even moderately steep, and the snow is deep—especially where a lot of dry powder falls because skis float better (that is, they don't sink as deeply) in light powder than do snowshoes by virtue of distributing your weight over more surface area. Basic touring skis are popular because they'll get you around on easy to moderately steep terrain. To ski steeper backcountry slopes, you'll need telemark or alpine touring ski gear and the skills for those two styles of skiing—both of which are too complex to cover here (see Appendix B).

Ski touring backcountry trails is different from doing it on the groomed trails of a cross-country skiing resort. Unlike the manicured snow of groomed trails, snow in the backcountry can be deep. It may vary in condition from one spot to another: firm and sometimes icy here, deep and light over there, a crust that

Snowshoes Vs. Skis

Trying to decide between snowshoes and skis? Each has advantages and disadvantages, so the choice comes down to trade-offs, personal preference, and where you're going.

Many winter hikers, from novices to the experienced, prefer snowshoes because they can step into them and go, whereas even ski touring easy terrain requires some practice. Snowshoes are more "agile" than skis: You can go up and down steep slopes on narrow trails in places that skis cannot. Decent backcountry snowshoes grip hard, icy snow better than skis. In difficult snow conditions such as a breakable crust or wet, heavy, "mashed potatoes" snow snowshoes are more forgiving than skis.

Nevertheless, skis have significant advantages over snowshoes. Skis generally "float" better in deep, light snow than snowshoes. They are faster (provided you're on terrain that's appropriate for skis or simply that the hills are not steeper than you're able to ski). Skiing is less strenuous than snowshoeing because you're shuffling your feet along rather than lifting them with each stride. You can go farther on skis than on snowshoes without tiring as quickly.

Ultimately, if you become proficient with both skis and snowshoes, you'll expand your winter horizons with the ability to choose one or the other depending on the terrain you'll encounter on a particular outing, how far you want to go, the snow conditions that day, and which of these incredibly fun activities you feel like doing that day.

Ice: The Bane of Skis & Snowshoes

Ice forming on the bottom of snowshoes or touring skis or snow freezing to them will create many problems for you and presents probably the biggest headache associated with either piece of gear. If you get water or wet snow under a snowshoe's cleat, it can freeze solid, often in a round shape like a baseball, which may send you sliding or tumbling on a bad fall. Similarly, allowing the underside of a ski to contact water or wet snow can result in it freezing in a flat strip or a ball of snow or ice, which sticks to the ground snow, preventing your ski from gliding. The best strategy is to avoid getting the bottom of snowshoes or skis wet: When you encounter water, carry them across. If you do get the bottoms wet, remove and dry them (in sunshine or with a cloth) before they freeze. If ice or snow freezes to them, scrape it off the ski, or hit the side of your snowshoe with a ski pole or against a tree trunk to dislodge the ice.

If the temperature rises above freezing or the snow is wet, if may be impossible to prevent snow or ice freezing to the bottom of snowshoes or skis; consider whether it's easier to carry them rather than to wear them. Otherwise, just live with the problem and continue on—it's part of the challenge of winter.

occasionally collapses under your weight along one stretch, and perhaps wet and heavy farther ahead. High drifts might form across the trail. While on a popular trail, you might have the tracks of previous skiers to follow, wind-blown snow may fill in tracks, or you may find no tracks and have to break your own trail through deep snow.

The upshot is that when ski touring in the backcountry, you have to be prepared for anything—and you need equipment that can handle the greater range of potential snow conditions (see Chapter 4). The skinny skis and lightweight bindings and boots used on groomed trails at a Nordic resort might work fine on an easy backcountry trail; but those skis and bindings are not made for the greater stresses that skiing ungroomed snow can place on them, and those boots lack the warmth and water resistance you'll want for skiing untracked snow, when your boots will often be covered by snow.

Touring skis are wider (roughly 80 to 90 mm near the tips) and heavier (five pounds or more per pair) than skinny cross-country skis, which helps in breaking trail and controlling the skis when going downhill in untracked snow. Some have metal edges, which help the skis grip and break through snow. Touring skis come in two types: waxable and waxless. Waxable skis are faster and grip better in many snow conditions than waxless skis, provided you apply the correct wax for the air temperature (sometimes trickier than it may seem). However, you have to wax frequently—before each use and sometimes more than once on an outing. Waxless skis use plastic bottoms with fish scale patterns for traction on snow, instead of wax. They are common because they handle the variety of snow conditions well and don't require constant waxing. Fish scales and wax grip well enough for climbing easy hills, but for steeper uphills, you'll either herringbone or side step up.

When considering how long a ski you need, consider two factors: (1) the snow conditions you'll typically encounter and (2) your skill level on skis. You can get recommendations on ski length for your body weight from the ski manufacturer or the retailer where you purchase skis—the more ski area (length and width) beneath you, the more flotation the ski can provide (that is, the less your skis will sink into the snow). You need less ski to stay atop heavy, firm snow (as is common near the coasts) than in light, powder snow (common in dry climates like the Rockies). If the trails you'll ski are popular and likely to have a track laid down by previous skiers, you'll have firm snow underfoot. The shorter the skis, the greater the agility and control you'll have on them.

Other Gear

You already know the famous "Ten Essentials" of hiking:
1. Navigation (map and compass)
2. Sun protection (sunglasses and sunscreen)
3. Insulation (extra clothing)
4. Illumination (headlamp or flashlight)
5. First-aid supplies
6. Fire (firestarter and matches/lighter)
7. Repair kit and tools (including knife)
8. Nutrition (extra food)
9. Hydration (extra water)
10. Emergency shelter

In winter, especially on daylong outings, this list necessarily expands. Without lip balm, for instance, your lips may dry up and, if it's cold and windy, may be bleeding by the time you get home. An emergency whistle makes a lot of sense, and a space blanket is so tiny and weightless that there's no reason to leave it at home. How much other emergency gear to carry—sleeping bag and pad, space blanket, bivy bag, stove, fuel, cook pot, a basic repair kit—comes down to choosing between the relative safety of traveling lighter and faster or slower and better equipped. On certain hikes, those things belong in your pack, and you should keep them on the master checklist of winter hiking gear that you consult when deciding what to take on a given day.

The potential winter gear list grows longer still—again, depending on your destination's terrain. If there's any chance of avalanche, mandatory safety gear includes an avalanche transceiver (or beacon), a backcountry shovel, and an avalanche probe. A transceiver is worn by every party member, and it is turned on and kept in transmit mode at all times during the day; should someone get caught in an avalanche, the other party members switch their transceivers to receive to help them locate the victim. Everyone also carries a shovel, and ideally there's more than one probe in the group, to help pinpoint a buried victim's location and dig him or her out (hopefully, in time to save the person). Presumed in this discussion is that you'll get proper training in how to evaluate avalanche conditions and use a transceiver, shovel, and probe before going into avalanche terrain. See Chapter 4 and the appendixes for more information on avalanche safety and training resources.

Technology has given us a few more gear choices when heading into the backcountry: a Global Positioning System (or GPS) receiver, an altimeter, and a cellular phone.

A **GPS receiver** picks up signals from satellites to locate your position more precisely than is usually possible with a map and compass, unless you're in a place marked on the map, such as a trail junction (see Chapter 4). However, a GPS unit cannot substitute for good map-and-compass skills—indeed, a GPS receiver communicates your position using a coordinates system like longitude and latitude, so you still have to apply that information to a map to determine your location. A GPS unit can be tremendously helpful in terrain that does not offer many landmarks to help you identify your location, especially in winter, when trails and trail markers can be buried under snow and navigation becomes more challenging than in summer.

An **altimeter** reads barometric pressure to calculate your altitude above sea level, making it valuable in mountains as another tool that can help identify your location (see Chapter 4). Altimeters are generally considered vital when climbing a big peak but not necessary for most winter hiking, especially on trails.

A cellular phone is not a piece of gear that can directly assist you, but if you're in a backcountry area where you're able to get a cell signal, the phone can greatly reduce the time it takes to get assistance to you when it's needed. Some traditionalists insist cell phones don't belong in the backcountry, for legitimate aesthetic reasons. Others argue there's no reason not to take anything that's easily portable and could potentially make the difference between someone living and dying. Make your own decision about the ethics of carrying a cell phone. Personally, although I generally do not carry a cell phone in the backcountry at any time of year—because most of the places I go wouldn't receive a cell signal anyway—I have used cell phones in emergencies in the mountains and been glad I had one. Moreover, I've yet to meet anyone who's used a cell phone successfully in an emergency and said later that they wished they hadn't had the phone.

However, responsible cell phone users should respect that many people go into the backcountry in part to escape the modern world and therefore refrain from using a cell phone except in an emergency or at least for a nonemergency call when another party is within earshot or sight. Hey, if you can't go hiking for a few hours without talking on the phone, you should rethink why you're going hiking in the first place. Remember to keep the phone turned off to preserve its batteries, and bear in mind that in most backcountry areas, you won't pick up a cell signal.

Traveling Light Vs. Safety

Your three-season hiking experience has taught you that choosing what to carry on an outing is subjective and varies depending on where you're going, how long you'll be gone, the weather, how far into the backcountry you'll be, the condition of the route, and how well you know that area. And having read this far, you're now anticipating that I'm going to suggest that in winter, much of this preparation is similar, yet you must take this intellectual process a step farther. You're right.

On a short winter hike, in good weather, on a good trail where you'll get at most a mile or two from the nearest road, you obviously don't need to be outfitted for an expedition: A little extra clothing, food, and water will suffice. The equation changes significantly on more committing, all-day trips deep into the backcountry. When you'll be hours from the nearest road in winter, it's prudent to carry what you'll need to survive an unplanned night outside. That may include any or all of the following:

▲ At least two reliable flashlights or headlamps and extra batteries (check the batteries before you head out)

▲ A sleeping bag rated for winter (roughly five degrees Fahrenheit to twenty degrees below Fahrenheit, depending on normal nighttime temperatures), or one rated for relatively cold temperatures (ten degrees to fifteen degrees), that will be more lightweight and compact than a winter bag and will probably enable you to survive the night, albeit not with a good night's sleep

▲ A **bivy** (or bivouac) **bag,** essentially an outer bag, usually W-B, inside which you slide your sleeping bag to keep yourself dry and protected from the wind

▲ A sleeping pad, to insulate yourself from the cold ground—vital to staying warm. A removable back pad in a pack might fill this role minimally, or even a foam pad cut short to reduce its bulk and weight.

▲ A backcountry stove, fuel, and a small cook pot, which at the least will enable you to melt snow for drinking water. A hot drink makes a big difference when you're stuck outside all night in winter.

▲ A lightweight, portable backcountry shovel for everything from building a snow shelter to rescuing an avalanche victim

▲ A small, basic repair kit that contains replacement parts and tools for fixing critical gear (such as your pack, ski bindings, snowshoes, stove)

How much to carry boils down to choosing between traveling as lightly as possible and, at the other extreme, being as prepared as possible for any circumstance.

Keeping your pack light allows you to move more quickly—valuable should the weather change abruptly or the hike prove to be more challenging than antici- pated. A light pack reduces to some extent the chances you'll slip, stumble, or fall. It's also easier on your body and more enjoyable. On the other hand, carrying emergency gear prepares you for the worst. There exist no hard-and-fast rules about what to carry on a winter hike. As stressed in Chapter 1 (see "Deciding Where to Go"), develop your skills in a steady progression, without biting off more than you can chew, and let experience tell you what you need in your pack.

Chapter 3

Water and Food

We all know the sermon about pouring enough water and food into our bellies to keep our bodies hydrated and fueled while hiking. Most of us know what it's like to have bonked—run out of gas—on a hike because we didn't have enough food along, or to have run out of water and become so dehydrated that our minds concentrate on nothing but finding that next drink of water.

Food and water take on a heightened urgency when the thermometer slips downward—and the colder it gets, the more fuel your body demands. Think about it this way: When you're hiking on a day that's seventy-five degrees, your body requires enough **calories** to produce the energy to power your body through the hike. When you're hiking in fifteen-degree weather, your body needs calories not only to produce the energy for walking but also to produce enough heat to keep you warm. And remember, in winter you're often wearing heavier boots and perhaps skis or snowshoes and carrying a heavier pack, meaning the hiking itself may be more physically demanding than in summer and thus may require more energy.

Drink Heavily; Be a Glutton

Water is the foundation of all life. It comprises the bulk of our bodies. Our cells cannot function properly without enough of it—water helps maintain proper pressure in our cells, which enables them to metabolize nutrients. Water keeps our

Backcountry skiers stop for a drink and lunch in Idaho's Sawtooth Mountains.

kidneys functioning. **Dehydration** causes a decrease in our blood volume, which results in less oxygen reaching our muscles and thus cramps and soreness during or after a hike. Sweating depletes our bodies of sodium and creates an imbalance in electrolytes. Without replacing that sodium and maintaining a balance of electrolyte minerals (sodium, potassium, magnesium, and calcium), our muscles won't contract and relax properly.

The average adult needs to drink about two liters of water per day when sedentary. That's how much a couch potato should drink. Physical activity increases our fluid needs by 50, 100, or even 200 percent, depending on factors like how hard we're working and for how long, the air temperature, humidity level, and our exposure to the sun. Big people need more water than smaller people.

Thirst is not a good indicator of when it's time to drink—by the time your brain registers thirst, you're well on the road to dehydration. Drink before you get thirsty. In winter, how much we perspire isn't a good litmus test of how much we need to drink either: In the cold, dry air of winter, we may not perspire much, but our bodies are losing fluids faster than we think through urination, our skin, and especially our breath. At any time of year, the best way to know you're drinking enough is the need to urinate regularly and having clear urine; if it's yellow or darker, you're dehydrated (see Chapter 6).

Consuming fluids frequently while hiking is the formula for staying hydrated. The only way to do that is to have water immediately accessible while hiking (see Chapter 2); if you have to stop and remove your pack to drink, you'll drink less often. Drinking a large amount infrequently will not achieve the same result: Your body can only absorb water at a rate of roughly one liter to one and a half liters per hour. Any surplus you drink above your body's ability to absorb and use it will simply leave your body in your urine. I keep a casual eye on my watch and remind myself to drink several gulps of water every 15 to 30 minutes on the trail. Over the course of several hours of hiking, I'll drink two to three liters, or more if I'm working hard.

From personal experience, I think it's safe to estimate your body needs up to 50 percent more fuel for a hike of comparable distance and time in winter than in summer. The average woman, when sedentary, burns 2100 calories a day—or an average of 87.5 calories per hour, though that hourly figure doesn't take into account the higher rate of calorie consumption when we're awake compared with when asleep. A sedentary man burns around 2800 calories per day, or 116.7 calories per hour. That's without any exertion.

Now throw into that equation a hike uphill with a pack weighing ten to twenty pounds. A 35-year-old woman who's 5 feet, 5 inches tall and weighs 130 pounds will burn 1705 calories in just 4 hours. A 5-foot, 9-inch man weighing 150 pounds, carrying the same pack on the same hike, will burn 2054 calories in 4 hours. If we (somewhat unscientifically) compare those numbers with the minimum 466.7 calories that the man would have burned if sedentary for those 4 hours, and the minimum 350 calories the woman would have burned, we can roughly calculate that hiking increased the fuel needs of the man by a factor of more than four, and the woman by a factor of nearly five.

Those figures assume moderate temperatures. Factor in my estimate of needing up to 50 percent more calories in winter compared with summer, and we find the man burning up to about 3000 calories on that 4-hour hike and the woman burning more than 2400 calories. Double the hiking time to 8 hours, and we're looking at about 6000 calories burned off in the man's body, and nearly 5000 calories in the woman. Need to drop a few extra pounds? Hiking in winter looks like an efficient way to accomplish that, doesn't it?

But don't treat winter hiking like a weight-loss program—you'll probably shed some pounds even while eating as much as you can on a hike, because let's face it, it would be quite a challenge to actually consume a surplus of calories when you're taking a substantial day hike in winter.

What happens if you don't eat and drink enough? You'll notice pronounced physical reactions to the calorie deficit. Your energy level will plunge quickly and dramatically. You'll suddenly feel chilled, from toes and fingers right to your body's core. Your mood will sour and you may feel like you don't want to be out there. Not only will that kind of physical reaction put a downer on your hike, but not being warm enough or having the energy you need can create a dangerous situation in winter if you're some distance into the backcountry. The lesson is clear: Be a glutton and drink heavily.

Care for a Sip of Ice Block?

The coincidence of physics that gave water a freezing temperature that's tolerable for humans is quite convenient, when you think about it. If, instead of thirty-two degrees Fahrenheit, water froze at, say, thirty-two degrees *below* Fahrenheit, then few of us would enjoy skiing or snowshoeing; few of us would even see snow or ice in our lifetimes. We should rejoice in the fact that water freezes at a temperature that, when dressed properly, we can find comfortable.

The one inconvenient thing about the freezing temperature of water is, well, its predisposition to freezing in freezing temperatures such as when we're out winter hiking. We have to take steps to prevent our water or any drink, including electrolyte-replacement drinks, from freezing. We also have to be concerned about the cap on our water bottles, or the hose and mouthpiece on our hydration system, freezing shut (see the sidebar entitled "Water Bottles and Hydration Systems").

Even a little insulation slows the freezing process. Water inside a sealed plastic bottle won't immediately begin to freeze if left out in air at exactly thirty-two degrees Fahrenheit; it will take some time for the first ice crystals to form on the water's surface. Stick that bottle inside a bottle insulator—much like a beer "cozy," but with a zippered lid to seal it up tight (they're inexpensive and available through many outdoor gear retailers)—or put the bottle inside your pack, and you've insulated it a little better and further slowed the freezing process. Wrap it in extra clothing, especially a good insulator like fleece, and you'll delay freezing even longer. Carry bottles upside down, so that ice begins forming in the bottom of the bottle rather than at the top, and you can still drink from a partly frozen bottle.

Water Bottles and Hydration Systems

You've probably used traditional water bottles and so-called hydration packs, or packs with a bladder carried in a sleeve inside the pack, with a hose extending over your shoulder and a bite valve at the end of the hose. Which to carry in winter? The convenience of a hydration pack—the great advantage of being able to drink anytime without stopping to take a drink—is not lost in moderate freezing temperatures, provided your hydration pack is designed for the cold. Those designs usually involve insulating the hose and bite valve; the bladder is close enough to your body that it shouldn't freeze. Having quick and easy access to water means you'll drink frequently, and hydration packs hold enough water for several hours of hiking. However, the disadvantages of these packs are that you can't see how much water you have left in the bladder without opening the pack and pulling the bladder out of its sleeve. You also can't use them in deep cold because the hose or bite valve will probably freeze at some point (especially if you're out all day and exposed to strong wind). You can thaw a bite valve in your mouth, but thawing a frozen hose takes more time—you'll have to tuck it inside your jacket for a while, but it could freeze again.

Water bottles gain some edge over hydration packs in winter because of the latter's risk of freezing. It's easier to prevent a water bottle from freezing and to thaw it if it does. In freezing temperatures, use only wide-mouth bottles like the popular Nalgene brand bottles made of hard plastic with screw-top caps. Wide-mouth bottle caps don't freeze as quickly as a bottle with a small mouth and cap. Nalgenes and similar bottles can hold a boiling liquid, and are marked off in metric and English measures, another convenience. Unless you're concerned about the water freezing solid (which can happen in temperatures in the teens or lower), carry it in a pocket on your pack that you can reach while hiking to ensure that you drink often (see "Care for a Sip of Ice Block?").

Cheaper plastic drink bottles bought in stores, which you might reuse in summer, are not a good choice in winter. They often have small mouths that freeze easily, and their plastic will crack more readily than a Nalgene bottle if the water inside freezes.

The lower the temperatures, of course, the faster water freezes. Somewhere around the low teens Fahrenheit, water starts freezing relatively quickly even inside a bottle insulator. Then you have to introduce heat to retard the freezing process. Your body is the only reliable, constant heat source accompanying you on most winter hikes. Pack your water supply (whether bottles or a bladder) close to your body inside your pack. You can also fill your bottles with boiling water (and a tea bag, hot chocolate, or some other drink) at home before the hike; then you'll have a nice, hot drink on the trail, and you can further delay it from freezing.

Treating Backcountry Water

If you're going to rely on backcountry sources of water—assuming they're not all frozen and buried under a thick layer of snow—you must know that, unfortunately, deep cold does not rid backcountry water sources of the tiny creatures that can raise havoc in our gastrointestinal tracts. Those creatures are the waterborne parasites *Giardia lamblia* and *Cryptosporidium,* or "crypto." If ingested, the former can cause *giardiasis,* also known as "backpacker's diarrhea." The latter has been identified by the federal Centers for Disease Control and Prevention as a major health risk to those who spend time in the woods. Crypto is easily transmitted in drinking water or from an infected hiking partner's dirty hands. If you drink untreated backcountry water, you risk swallowing both of these microscopic parasites. Symptoms appear one to three weeks (an average of nine days) after ingesting the parasite and include loose and foul-smelling stool, cramps, rotten-egg burps, and a loss of energy, appetite, and weight. Giardiasis can be treated with antibiotics, but there is no medication to treat crypto. Your body has to rid itself of the parasite, and that takes time.

Still, the incidence of health problems related to these two parasites is low. That's no doubt due to the fact that many hikers treat their water or simply carry all the water from home that they'll need on a day hike—the best strategy for day hikers. If circumstances require you to drink water from a backcountry source, consider the following options for treating it: boiling, filtration, or halogenation.

Boiling is a proven infallible method of purifying water to make it safe to drink. You need only bring water to the boiling point to purify it—there's no need to boil it for several minutes, a common misconception, and sustained boiling merely consumes fuel that you might need later. Boiling obviously requires that you carry a stove, fuel, and pot, which winter hikers might bring along as emergency gear on a long trek into the mountains but wouldn't lug on every hike. Boiling is also time-consuming, and in winter you can get cold sitting around waiting for water to boil.

Filtering water is convenient for hikers and effective when the filtering device removes protozoa, bacteria, and viruses. However, freezing temperatures render a filter useless and could crack or otherwise damage the unit. Filters are not a viable option in winter.

Halogens—iodine and chlorine—offer the easiest water-treatment method for winter hikers, and I prefer the latter for treating water on the trail at any time of year. Treating water with chlorine dioxide involves simply mixing several drops of two liquids together in a cap, waiting several minutes, then dumping the mixture into your water bottle. Chlorine dioxide is effective at inactivating protozoa, bacteria, and viruses in water.

Iodine comes in tablet, crystal, and liquid forms, is lightweight and cheap, and involves dropping the iodine into your water bottle and waiting at least 10 minutes. Use two iodine tablets in cold water. After the tablets dissolve, loosen the cap slightly and shake the bottle to swish treated water through the bottle cap and screw threads. Wait 20 to 30 minutes after dissolving the tablets before adding something to improve the taste, like a powder drink mix or an iodine neutralizer.

Be aware, however, that recent studies suggest iodine is less effective at killing protozoa like *Giardia,* and there are outstanding questions about iodine's effect on humans. Halogens also do nothing to improve the quality of murky water, although you can rid water of much sediment by allowing it to settle for a while in a bottle or pot, then carefully pouring out the clear water before dumping the sediment that's settled at the bottom.

What to Eat

Here's where winter hiking gets fun. Think about it: In winter, you're hiking either in a freezer, or (if the temperature's above freezing) in a cold refrigerator. The ambient air temperature greatly expands your choices of foods you can bring on an all-day hike. Chocolate won't melt, a stick of pepperoni won't get greasy—heck, you could bring a turkey club sandwich, cup of yogurt, any kind of beverage, even a slice of apple pie or milk and cookies, if you want (provided that you protect certain foods from getting crushed in your pack by padding them with clothing or using a plastic vacuum-sealed container). Rather than worrying about perishables spoiling, you only have to worry about them freezing or, with a block of cheese, getting kind of crumbly. Protect any food that could freeze the same way you would protect it from the heat in summer, by wrapping it in insulation (like fleece) inside your pack. If it's cold outside, you might even place it close to your body inside your pack. Put lightweight, nonbulky items that can get hard in the cold, such as energy bars, in a pocket to let your body heat warm them a short while before you eat them.

Hot foods like soup are a welcome addition to lunchtime on a cold day. A thermos will keep liquids hot for hours, so you can make it at home and not bother firing up a stove in the backcountry.

In winter, though, it can be difficult to do a lot of outdoor food preparation with your hands—fingers get cold quickly. A task like peeling an orange becomes unpleasant (and many fruits, like bananas, will go bad quickly in the cold). In short, think about how much work with your hands will be required of any foods you pack for a winter hike; keep it simple, and do as much food preparation as possible in the warmth of your home before your hike (slice up the cheese beforehand, etc.). Otherwise, stick with snack and energy bars, nuts, dried fruit, meats that require no preparation (jerky or pepperoni), cheese, chocolate, breads or bagels, crackers—or treats that don't require any work, like that slice of pie.

Eat smartly on a hike—your body needs the energy—following standard nutritional guidelines that call for a diet comprised half of carbohydrates, 30 percent of fats, and 20 percent of proteins. Fats contain about twice the calories per pound of carbohydrates or protein and provide the slow-burning fuel that keeps your body moving and keeps you warm in the cold. Fats are found in cheese, chocolate, canned meat or fish, pepperoni, sausage, and nuts or nut products like peanut butter. Proteins—vital to cell health—are found in cheese, beans, nuts, and grains like crackers and breads.

Fill up your internal fuel tank with a good dinner the evening before your big winter hike, following those dietary guidelines, so that you'll have the energy you'll need on the trail. Within 30 minutes to 2 hours after concluding your hike, eat a meal—or at least a good snack—in the 50-30-20 proportions of carbohydrates to fat to protein, like a bagel with cream cheese. You'll be hungry by then—your body signaling for what it needs—and that posthike food will replenish depleted energy stores.

Lastly, eat as much as you feel like eating while on the trail. Don't worry about overeating out there—better to do that than to get lethargic and cold. If you want to crunch numbers, the respected National Outdoor Leadership School (NOLS) uses the following rough formula when planning food for program participants: 1.5 to 2 pounds of food provides 2500 to 3000 calories. But rest assured, in winter we rarely wonder when it's time to eat—our bodies let us know.

How Much Water and Food to Bring

When it comes to the question of how much weight we're carrying on our backs, hikers and backpackers have gotten smarter in recent years: We try to go with as light a load a possible without compromising safety. Although you should adhere to that go-light philosophy in winter, too, the goal is a little harder to achieve in the cold months. You're already carrying more clothing, you may be carrying emergency gear such as a bag and pad, and you might have specialized gear such as an ice ax and crampons. We don't tend to head into the mountains for an all-day hike in winter with just six or eight pounds on our backs, as we might get away with in summer. (Ultimately, the best preparation for inherently heavier loads in winter is to make sure you're in the best possible physical condition.)

It becomes more important in winter to carry some extra food and water, just in case you're out there longer than anticipated, especially when you'll get more than a mile or two from the nearest road in terrain that doesn't permit you to move fast. Again, experience will teach you how much to carry. On those inaugural big winter day hikes, pack a few liters of water (unless you plan to boil or treat water during the day) and an extra stash of food beyond what you plan and expect to eat. An extra liter of water weighs just a bit more than two pounds; most energy bars weigh just two or three ounces. The additional weight will seem insignificant if you're out in the woods hours later than planned with a rumbling belly.

Chapter 4

Getting Around

T his chapter's title implies a nice simplicity to this business of getting from point A to point B in winter. If that were true, this chapter might be much shorter than it is; but we'd also lose some of the challenges that make hiking in winter, in many ways, a more exciting and satisfying experience than it is at any other time of year.

This chapter covers everything from the fundamentals of using a map and compass to the terrain hazards exclusive to the winter environment—the "winter environment" certainly extending beyond the calendar dates of winter in many mountain ranges. You may already have some of the skills and knowledge covered here, but you might also find a refresher course in areas like navigating with a map and compass valuable as you prepare for adventures in the forests and mountains in winter.

The Challenges of Winter

The logical place to begin a discussion about "getting around" in winter is with the aspects of hiking that are directly affected by freezing temperatures and with the areas that have snow or ice on the ground.

Trails

Following a snow-covered trail can be as simple as staying in a track (or trough) broken out by previous hikers, snowshoers, or skiers, and as confounding as scanning

Traveling through the backcountry in winter presents many navigational challenges, as these skiers discover on a multi-day trip in Yellowstone National Park.

a forest or open meadow with your eyes and, despite thinking or knowing that the trail is there somewhere, having it all look the same to you. As discussed in Chapter 1, popular trails are easier to follow in winter than little-used trails, because staying on an unbroken trail can be extremely challenging. Just a few inches of snow can obscure the footpath. Snow that's several feet deep may bury blazes on trees and raise you into the forest canopy—the branches overhanging the trail that are high overhead in summer—making it hard or impossible to discern the trail corridor through the forest. Most trail maintenance occurs in late spring and summer, so trees blown down across trails by winter storms will be there for weeks or months.

When following a trail, whether you're on a track that previous hikers have broken in the snow or breaking your own track, remain vigilant for signs of the trail such as blazes, cairns, other markers, and the trail corridor through the trees. Having a broken track to follow does not guarantee that whoever laid the track stayed on the actual trail. You can daydream while hiking a trail in summer, but in winter, a spell of daydreaming can take you off course quickly.

When following a firm, broken track through the snow, it's often possible to remove your snowshoes and hike in boots without punching deeply into the snow—known as **postholing**—plus carrying the snowshoes on your pack is less tiring than lifting their weight with each stride. If, however, the traction your boots get on the trail's packed snow is so poor that your feet slip or feel like they're treading snow with each step, it may be less strenuous and faster to wear your snowshoes for their traction.

Skiing, on the other hand, unless the terrain is prohibitively steep, is much faster and less strenuous than hiking in boots, because you shuffle your feet on skis, whereas you lift your feet when walking. A broken track makes skiing that much easier and faster. On flat to gently rolling terrain, there's rarely a reason to carry your skis.

When no blazes or markers are visible in the direction you're walking, turn around and look for markers in the opposite direction—seeing one will at least confirm you're on the trail and seeing more than one may show you the trail's line and suggest the direction it leads.

Watch for the trail's corridor through the trees, which is generally at least two feet wide. When snow covers the ground, it's easy to mistake an opening in the trees for the trail corridor, so remember that a trail will have no vegetation growing within it and usually takes a logical and generally straight course (that is, it doesn't constantly zigzag or wander up and down slopes when contouring around them is the obvious best way to go).

A fresh snow may visually obscure a previous track, but that track still exists beneath the fresh white. The previous track will still support your weight much better than untracked snow off the trail. In other words, your boots, snowshoes, or skis won't sink as deeply into the snow while you're on the trail. If you suddenly notice yourself sinking more deeply, you may have wandered off the trail.

Off-Trail

Going off-trail is fun and a fast way to find solitude, even in a popular area. Depending on many variables, including the snowpack condition, terrain, and density of the vegetation cover, winter may make going off-trail more difficult than sticking with the trail or more direct and easier. There's little reason to follow a trail's myriad switchbacks down a hillside, for instance, when you can point your skis downhill and just go. However, often the difficulty will ratchet up. Once you head off-trail, you'll break your own track through the snow, which is more strenuous and slower than following an existing track. Even the most rugged of trails take the most navigable terrain in an area, so you might surmise that by going off-trail, you may be getting into terrain that the trail builders wanted to avoid because of its obstacles or difficulty. Carry and frequently consult a detailed map, and keep in mind that if you're far from a trail, the likelihood of someone finding you is slim. Before leaving a trail behind, remember that making forward progress is more difficult than when following a trail, because you have to find your way rather than simply following a trail: Don't start bushwhacking thinking that you're going to save time. That said, I've had some of my most satisfying backcountry experiences when I've wandered away from the trail in winter.

Leaving the trail in winter increases the challenges of finding your way around.

Time and Distances

What happened to the time? If you find that question forming in your mind some late afternoon in the backcountry in winter, take consolation in knowing you're in the company of many who came before you. Three factors collaborate to try to catch winter hikers out as darkness looms: (1) days are short, especially in early winter; (2) conditions (snow, trail, weather) may slow you significantly, meaning it takes longer than anticipated to cover the distance you've planned; and (3) travel on foot is often strenuous, possibly causing you or someone in your party to fatigue sooner than expected, which will further slow you down. The answer? Plan conservatively, know how far your party is capable of going, and have alternate plans in case you need to turn around or cut the day short. Be aware of what time the sun sets, and keep an eye on your watch.

Snow, Ice, and Mud

The ground surface assumes many different faces in winter. In summer it's pretty much either dirt or rock, wet or dry, yet in winter it can be any of those combinations, as well as ice and the many forms of snow. Some of these surfaces can be as easy and fast to travel on as a dry trail of firm dirt is in summer, whereas others can make every step forward extremely arduous—a big part of the reason that travel times vary so greatly in winter. The following is an overview of frozen surfaces you might encounter and suggestions for how to deal with them.

Ice or a *firm crust* of snow that does not collapse beneath your weight are both fast surfaces for self-powered travel but also slippery and potentially dangerous. I'll include in this category the snow condition mountaineers call "Styrofoam" for its similarity in consistency to that man-made substance; you'll see mountaineers say that word with a smile, because crampons bite well into Styrofoam snow, and it holds a person's weight, allowing them to move fast up or down. Styrofoam, ice, and an unbreakable crust usually require the use of some type of crampon—the steeper the ground, the more substantial the crampon is needed, and you may also need an ice ax for safety. You can move quickly over firm snow on snowshoes or skis, provided the terrain isn't too steep: As the ground angle increases, you'll lean with increasing force on ski edges to get traction, until the skis become more of a liability than an advantage. Snowshoes will get you through steeper terrain than skis, but it's important that the snowshoes have a beefy cleat and that you use it effectively; and going downhill in snowshoes on ice or a hard crust is more treacherous than going uphill.

A *breakable crust* is the bane of winter travelers whether hiking in boots (with or without crampons), skiing, or snowshoeing. Arguably worse is when the crust sometimes supports your weight, and sometimes collapses under you, because you never know when you'll go through; there's a constant danger of a debilitating injury like hyperextending a knee as you tumble forward. Breakable crust demands caution and may slow your progress dramatically. How consistently the crust breaks, and the firmness of the snow underneath the crust (it's often sugar snow—see the next entry), will determine whether you're better off keeping your snowshoes or skis on or removing them. Usually the flotation either provides is beneficial, possibly reducing the number of times you break through the crust. However, some people—especially anyone inexperienced on skis or snowshoes—may feel more comfortable and safer without them, especially on steep terrain.

Unconsolidated snow—sometimes called **sugar** or **T.G. snow** (the latter for "temperature gradient," a reference to the fact that it can form when the snow cover is relatively shallow and there's a pronounced difference in the temperature of the ground, which is always around freezing, and the temperature of the air immediately above the snow surface)—is basically snow that does not bond together after landing on the ground. A sugar snow layer may be anywhere from a few inches to several feet deep; it's not uncommon to find sugar snow beneath a breakable crust. The science of how snow transforms itself once on the ground is complex and of prime interest to anyone who may go into territory where avalanches can occur (see later); entire books have been written about it (see Appendix B). What the winter hiker needs to know is that this layer of sugarlike snow can make travel difficult and frustrating. Sugar snow won't hold your weight, and trying to get through it is like walking on a pile of ball bearings. It may be so light that your legs plunge in deeply even on snowshoes or skis. A sugar layer may only cover a limited area—perhaps on one slope but not on another slope with a different **aspect,** or that faces in a different compass direction—so if you encounter it, altering your course to a different aspect may get you onto better snow. If the sugar layer covers a vast area, you might want to turn around and go home.

Dry snow, as we all know, is the beautiful light powder that falls in fat, crystalline flakes, piles up on tree limbs, forms huge mushroom caps on boulders, and generally turns the backcountry into a stunning work of art in white. It falls during snowstorms with colder temperatures and has a lower moisture content than the wet snow that falls when the temperature is near freezing. Once on the ground, these fat flakes with their multiple points bond together well and gradually consolidate, so that the deeper you go into this snow, the denser it gets. This stuff is great for snowshoeing or skiing because you can move fairly easily through the upper layers, but the lower layers have consolidated enough to support a person's weight on skis or snowshoes (although you'll posthole to your crotch without one or the other).

Wet snow falls when the temperature is near freezing and is more common in maritime climates—near oceans and large lakes, both of which affect local weather patterns. It has a high moisture content, bonds well, and consolidates quickly into a solid snowpack (for example, the bulletproof snow commonly on the ground in the Northeast and the "Cascades cement" of the Pacific Northwest). It can offer good snowshoeing and ski touring while it's falling, and within a day or two you may even be snowshoeing or skiing right on top of the surface, or possibly even hiking in boots without the need for snowshoes or skis. The downside is its tendency to freeze to ice or form a crust that may be breakable or firm. Its high water content means that as temperatures creep above freezing in spring, it can sport a top layer of meltwater or slush or transform more thoroughly into a few feet or more soft, wet slush; moving through that stuff can be miserable. Similarly, the first snowfall of the season in many places, even drier climates, usually arrives in "warmer" temperatures near freezing, depositing a wet snow that, if deep enough, makes hiking in boots difficult but often has consolidated enough to support someone on snowshoes or skis.

Mashed potatoes snow is something you have to experience to fully appreciate. Backcountry skiers know it as heavy, half-frozen muck that's hard to ski through without falling—repeatedly. This stuff is aptly named, bearing a striking resemblance as it does to the stuff that we eat (albeit much colder). It forms when snow on the ground has been subjected to sustained temperatures above freezing and/or rain. It has a high water content and may clump up and stick to the bottom of skis or under snowshoe cleats. The only snow worse than mashed potatoes is a breakable crust.

No discussion of winter ground surfaces would be complete without mentioning *mud*. Mud happens. Mud is the universal, multiseason ground medium. Winter hikers may find it anytime from late autumn through early spring. You may have to plod through mud at lower elevations to reach snow at higher elevations. You'll survive it, of course. Just bear in mind that mud on your gear could freeze once you get higher up, so carry your skis or snowshoes through it so as not to get them wet. And remember that mud is one of the reasons God made gaiters, so put them on.

Lakes and Rivers

Water poses one of the greatest potential hazards in winter, and the dangers of lakes and rivers are similar and different.

Lakes and ponds in northern latitudes often freeze solidly, the ice going down a few feet or more in cold climates, thick enough to support a motor vehicle. Walking, skiing, or snowshoeing across a frozen lake can be not only much easier than following its shore but also enjoyable and scenic. However, wind patterns and underwater springs can create areas of thin ice that aren't always easy to detect, especially with any snow cover on the ice. Misjudge the thickness of ice and you or a companion could abruptly be in danger of drowning or experiencing hypothermia (see Chapter 6).

The thickness of ice on the same water body can vary greatly from one winter to the next, depending on the weather. For instance, an early-season snowfall may cover the ice before it had gotten thick, insulating it and preventing it from freezing as quickly as would uncovered water or ice. Freshwater ice will support a person's weight once it's between an inch and two inches thick. If the lake is on public land, ask the management agency about current ice conditions.

Wearing skis or snowshoes spreads your weight over a larger area of ice, reducing the chance of breaking through (Illustration 4-1). Snow atop the ice also helps disperse your weight. Spread your party out to avoid more than one person breaking through the ice.

Avoid known weak spots such as springs or anywhere streams enter and leave the lake. Be careful at narrow spots in a lake, where there can sometimes be a slight current.

As you cross a lake, look for dark areas ahead—they may indicate thin ice or water seeping up through a crack. Avoid objects in the ice such as rocks or logs, which radiate solar heat, creating a surrounding ring of weaker ice.

Probe the ice ahead of you with a ski pole. A solid "tick" indicates thick ice; a hollow "tock" suggests thin ice.

Trees often shield the south shore of a lake from direct winter sunlight, so you'll find the strongest ice there.

Animals offer clues about the ice: Fresh deer tracks usually indicate solid ice. Otter tracks tend to lead toward open water.

Carry something to help you "claw" your way out if you do fall in, like a small knife or a short screwdriver. If a companion goes in, don't approach the person too closely, but try to extend a rope or line to help pull him or her out.

Illustration 4-1: Crossing a frozen lake

Rivers and streams may or may not freeze solidly enough to travel on in winter. Fast-moving and steeply dropping water does not tend to freeze, whereas big, flat, slow rivers in cold climates often freeze solidly and make excellent highways for skiers, snowshoers, and sled dog teams. Many of the earlier guidelines for crossing a frozen lake also apply to rivers. Some other suggestions include the following:

▲ The thickness of ice on rivers and streams can vary greatly within a short distance because of currents or proximity to objects that radiate solar heat, like shoreline vegetation or logs and rocks. Watch constantly for weaknesses.

▲ Stay away from a river's main current, which tends to sweep to the far bank in each meander of the channel, because the ice may be thinnest under the fastest-moving water. Similarly, be aware of spots where wind may consistently blow across the river; wind can cause the ice to be thin or create open water.

▲ Crossing an open stream or creek in temperatures around or below freezing can be dangerous because of the imminent danger of hypothermia should you fall in. Avoid fording any moving water with a significant current that's more than knee deep, and certainly avoid any current strong enough to carry you downstream if you fall in, because hypothermia can quickly render your limbs useless. If there's any current, assume fording it may be harder than it looks. Don't look at it the same way you would in summer—the same current will often be more difficult in winter because of the likelihood that you'll lose sensation in your feet, and it's more dangerous because of the repercussions of falling in.

▲ Search the area for alternatives to fording, such as a natural bridge (although rocks and logs can be ice-covered or slick when wet or frozen). If your map shows a confluence of two tributaries upstream, go there to cross because each tributary presents an easier crossing than the single stream holding the same volume of water.

If you deem the crossing safe, follow these guidelines:

▲ Your feet will probably go numb before you finish the crossing; be prepared to warm them again on the other side. Protective footwear of some kind is imperative, but you want to keep your primary boots dry. If you don't have alternate footwear (for example, sneakers or sandals brought for this purpose), wear only a pair of socks (assuming little current and a soft river bottom); or if your primary boots have a removable insulated liner, remove the liner to keep it dry and ford the stream in your boot shells, and then dry them (and your feet) as thoroughly as possible on the other side. After dumping water out of the shells, it's sometimes easier to let the moisture that remains inside them freeze, then break up the ice and dump it out.

▲ Ford where the stream is wide and shallow or braided in multiple channels. Avoid big boulders, which can make a current unpredictable.

▲ Use trekking poles or walking sticks for balance. Loosen your pack straps and unfasten your hipbelt and chest strap, in case you fall in and need to quickly remove the pack. Look straight ahead while crossing, not down at the moving water, which can make you lose your balance. Probe ahead with your walking sticks, move just one foot or stick at a time, and don't rush. If necessary, cross with your companion(s), bracing against one another.

▲ Don't panic if you fall in. Get out of the water as quickly as possible, and change into dry clothes immediately. Don't change clothing in a cold wind—find a protected spot or erect a tent if necessary. If you're still cold once in dry clothing, get into a sleeping bag to warm up, eat some food, or have a hot drink.

The Hazards of Winter

Now that we've covered all the things that make getting around the backcountry in winter more challenging than in the other seasons, we'll get into the things that make it more dangerous and why and how to avoid them. Injuries resulting from the following are rare, especially among recreational winter hikers, snowshoers, and skiers who stay in wooded, gentle terrain, but it's wise to understand the dangers they pose and to recognize them when you're out there.

Avalanche

An **avalanche** is simply a significant volume of snow—sometimes many tons—releasing abruptly and falling rapidly downhill. They can occur spontaneously, but the victim or another party moving across unstable snow triggers many that result in injury to humans. This book doesn't cover this subject in sufficient depth to prepare you for travel in potential avalanche terrain (see Appendix B for recommended books). However, it's important that you have a fundamental understanding of where avalanches can occur—they don't just happen anywhere, anytime, and they do behave with some predictability.

First, they only occur on slopes angled between twenty-five degrees and fifty-five degrees but are infrequent on slopes of less than thirty degrees—which, as a point of reference, is the steepness of most ski resort black-diamond trails. (Avalanches don't happen at resorts because ski patrols bomb potential avalanche slopes to release new snow before skiers hit the slopes.) They are most common on open, treeless slopes during a heavy snowstorm (when snow accumulates at one inch per hour or faster) or within 24 hours of the storm ending. Winds greater than 15 mph can transport snow to the lee side of ridges, creating avalanche conditions. Long periods of cold nights can also transform the snow on the ground in complex ways that increase the risk of avalanche. Dense forest cover tends to "anchor" snow, even on steep slopes, preventing avalanches.

In short, stick to heavily wooded areas and avoid steep, open slopes during or immediately after a significant snowfall or times of heavy wind, and you'll be safe. Many winter-use trails avoid dangerous terrain. When in doubt, ask the management agency to recommend trails that are safe from avalanche hazard. If you want to venture above tree line, check on avalanche conditions; avalanche advisories are available in some areas.

Crevasses and Moats

Unless you're on a glacier, you won't likely run into a crevasse—a large crack in the glacier—that itself is a slowly moving river of ice. You may well see a moat, though, which poses a somewhat similar hazard (although moats are generally much smaller than crevasses). A **moat** is a trench that steadily widens and deepens as snow melts away from a cliff face or large boulder as a result of the heat of sunlight radiating off the rock. They may be a few feet to several feet across and deeper than they are wide. Moats form anywhere there is snow and an object radiating solar heat, and if you lose your footing or a ski edge above one, you may well crash suddenly down into it. The danger they pose is, obviously, a traumatic injury, but there's also a risk of hypothermia because it's usually much colder inside this hole than outside, and icy, melting water may be pouring into it. If the moat is deep, it can be difficult extracting a victim. Falls into moats almost invariably occur when someone attempts to hike or ski a slope above one. Be on the lookout for them and be careful when passing near or above one.

Falling Ice

This differs from avalanches in that I'm referring here to chunks and large blocks of ice breaking off of cliffs during periods of melting, or ice "chandeliers" falling out of trees during or after an ice storm. These can cause nasty injuries—deep, dull cuts; broken bones; head injury—and occasionally kill people. The danger of falling ice isn't limited to elite mountaineers: Plenty of winter hiking trails access mountain ravines and other areas where ice forms—and occasionally topples—from cliffs.

You can't anticipate when a huge block of ice will break off of a cliff, and the odds of this happening to you are pretty darn slim. But you can be aware of when you're below ice-clad cliffs and whether the temperature is above freezing or the cliffs are getting direct sunlight that's causing melting, which can occur from solar heat and radiation off rocks even if the temperature is slightly below freezing. Just keep your wits about you and don't hang around below cliffs when there's obviously ice melting from them. If there's been a major ice storm that has left the trees coated with ice—their branches drooping under the weight—that ice is going to come down sometime, probably within a day or two after the storm. Don't go out there until the ice has fallen to the ground, or if you do, wear a helmet and watch out.

Hidden Logs and Rocks

Big logs and rocks can lie just beneath the surface of the snow, posing a danger of broken bones and other serious injury to anyone moving fast and colliding with one. This is primarily a danger for backcountry skiers who gravitate to steeper slopes and ski fast downhill, but it can also happen to someone ski touring in rolling terrain who happens to gain a little speed going down a short hill. It's less of a risk to snowshoers because they generally don't gather that much momentum.

Although being on the trail isn't a guarantee of safety because trees do fall across trails, following a packed track reduces the risk significantly because it's unlikely your ski will slip underneath a buried log when you're atop a packed track. In general, watch for subtle high spots in the snow's surface that may signal a hidden log or boulder; similarly, slight depressions in the snow's surface may indicate a hole between boulders that can be equally hazardous should you plunge in abruptly and pitch forward.

Spruce Trap

These are one of those oddities about winter that many people would never anticipate but are a real hazard anytime you wander off the trail in a conifer forest where much snow has accumulated. A spruce trap occurs when a short spruce or other conifer tree gets completely buried under powder snow; because there's so much air and weak branches in the "trap," it cannot hold someone's weight as would normal, consolidated snow on the ground. You may be snowshoeing over what appears to be beautiful snow that's devoid of vegetation, pass unknowingly over a buried young conifer sapling, and suddenly plunge in up to your thighs or deeper. You'll find yourself swimming in bottomless snow with nothing underfoot to support your weight. An injury resulting directly from the fall into the trap is probably rare, but getting yourself out of it without help is difficult.

By staying on a trail, you'll avoid any danger of falling into a spruce trap, because trees don't grow in the trail. If you deliberately venture off-trail, spread out a bit and stay within earshot and sight of one another, in case someone goes in and needs help. Wearing clothing that's waterproof and close fitting will keep you relatively dry if you wind up in a trap.

Tree Well

This is a bowl-like depression encircling the base of a tree, caused by solar warmth radiating from the tree. Wells grow deeper and wider as the days get longer and warmer and the sun higher in the sky in late winter and spring. Tree wells are more common in open forest where the sun reaches the ground. Melting and freezing cycles can create a bulletproof shell of ice on the well's surface. Catch a ski edge or snowshoe on the lip of a well and you'll slam into the tree faster and harder than you thought possible. Avoiding tree wells is simple: Just avoid them. When skiing, control your speed. Be aware of when you're passing above tree wells and be careful.

A spruce trap can be difficult to extricate yourself from, as these two hikers discover in New Hampshire's White Mountains.

Undercut Snow

Snow on the ground can melt or get eroded from underneath by running water or solar warmth radiating from rocks and other objects. This is common in late winter and spring, and you may run into undercut snow well into summer at higher elevations. You may be walking atop a firm, solid snowpack and not realize that you've come upon a stretch of it that's melted out from underneath, leaving just a thin snow bridge that looks no different from above than the deep snowpack you've been on. Breaking through a snow bridge abruptly can result in a short fall or a drop of several feet; but however far the drop, its unexpectedness and the almost inevitable landing on rocks or some other uneven, hard ground can cause serious injury.

Watch vigilantly for the places where snow gets undercut, such as beside a creek or in a boulder field. Assume that if the temperature is above freezing and there are creeks or objects radiating solar heat nearby (rocks, trees, etc.), you're likely to encounter undercut snow. If you see any signs of undercut snow nearby, or see where people or large animals have broken through the snow, proceed with extra caution or consider turning back. Probe ahead with poles. Snowshoes and skis disperse your weight, reducing the chance you'll break through a snow bridge but may be inconvenient for other reasons (hard, uneven, and/or discontinuous snow cover, tricky footing amid boulders, etc.).

Finding Your Way

Sure, you've used a map and compass many times. You know how to figure out your direction of travel, where you are, and how to get where you want to be. Chances are, however, you've not often relied on the map and compass and your navigational skills to the degree that you may often call upon them when snow covers the ground. In summer, unless going off-trail, we typically consult our map only occasionally, perhaps at trail intersections, and our compass may make rare appearances outside of our packs. In winter, we cultivate a more intimate relationship with our map, and the compass and perhaps other navigational devices are kept handy and actually get used. So a refresher course in backcountry navigation is in order.

For starters, make sure you have a good map for winter backcountry travel. If you're not sure, reread the "Guidebooks and Maps" section of Chapter 1.

Map and Compass

The map and compass go hand in hand. If you have a good basic sense of direction and know the direction you've been traveling on a trail, then you may not need your compass to orient your map when you pull out the map to consult it. Like reading a street map, if you know your direction of travel, you can look at the map and determine, for instance, which way you need to turn at the trail intersection. If you know approximately where north is, you can roughly orient your map and identify major natural features, such as a nearby peak, cliff, or lake.

With snow on the ground, though, the trail (or trails) may not be visible. Snow conditions, blow downs, ice, and other variables beyond your control may force you to leave the trail and find your way navigating cross-country. For many reasons, you'll probably turn to your map and compass more often in winter than you do in summer.

When navigating by map and compass, begin by orienting your map, which simply means turning it so that its arrows showing the direction of true north and magnetic north on the map point in those actual directions. (This is easier to visualize if you use a map and compass while reading these instructions [Illustration 4-2].) Hold the map flat. Set your compass on the map, and align the long side of the compass, or the direction arrow on the compass base plate, with the line indicating magnetic north on the map. Make sure the north-south lines and arrow of the rotating faceplate on the compass point is in the same direction as the base plate's direction arrow and thus is in the same direction as the map's magnetic-north line. Then rotate the compass and map together until the red half of the needle sits squarely inside the faceplate arrow. The red end of the needle always points toward magnetic north. Your map is now oriented.

Once the map is oriented, terrain features depicted on it lie in the same direction relative to your position on the map as those features actually lie in relation to where you're standing (that is, the waterfall shown on the map as being on your left is there when you look left—assuming it's not obstructed by something else).

Orienting the map lets you take the information shown on the map and transfer it to your surroundings, giving you a sense of where you are. But if you have information that relies on you knowing the actual direction of a compass point—say, instructions from a guidebook telling you to walk due east or follow a bearing of 90° (which is due east)—you must understand declination and the difference between true north and magnetic north.

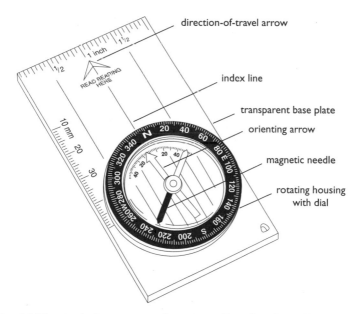

Illustration 4-2: The standard components of a compass (From Cox, Steven M., and Kris Fulsaas, eds. *Mountaineering: The Freedom of the Hills.* 7th ed. Seattle: The Mountaineers Books, 2003.)

True north is the direction to the North Pole. **Magnetic north** is the direction to the Earth's magnetic north pole, determined by the planet's magnetic field and located in Arctic Canada, south of the North Pole. A magnetized compass needle points to magnetic north rather than true north, and the declination of any particular spot on the planet is the angle of difference between the direction of true north and the direction of magnetic north, measured in degrees on a circle. The **declination** varies for different regions and is indicated on any good map. (For example, the declination in Colorado's Rocky Mountain National Park is 11.5° east, meaning that magnetic north lies 11.5° east of true north in that area.)

To compensate for declination, rotate the round faceplate dial on your compass—which is marked off in degrees—so that the small arrow or line (which doesn't move) above the faceplate dial points to the declination where you are (in Rocky Mountain National Park, that would be 11.5° east on the dial). With your compass corrected for declination, hold it flat in your hand, turn yourself until the colored end of the needle sits inside the faceplate arrow (or two parallel colored lines on some compasses). As long as you keep the colored end of the needle inside the faceplate arrow, north on the dial points to true north, south points south, east points east, and west points west. You can walk in any direction and know the compass direction and degree bearing (for instance, east is 90°, west is 270°, etc.) in which you're headed.

At times, you may have to follow a compass bearing to navigate cross-country from one point to another, a skill that's called on in winter when, for example, fog or falling snow obliterate the landscape (creating a "whiteout"; see Chapter 5), or when you've lost the trail but have some sense of your location and know where you want to go. The technique is called *following a bearing* because you're moving in the direction of a degree measure on the faceplate—if walking due south, for example, you're following a bearing of 180°.

These simple steps spell out how to take and follow a compass bearing:

1. Set the compass on the map with the base plate's direction arrows pointing from your position (on the map) to your destination.
2. Rotate the faceplate until the colored end of the needle is inside the north-south arrow on the faceplate and the needle and north-south arrow are pointing in the same direction—that is, the north-south arrow on the faceplate is pointing to magnetic north. Now you can put the map away.
3. With the compass held flat in your hand, the base plate direction arrow will point you toward your destination while you walk, provided you keep the north-south arrow on the faceplate pointing to magnetic north and don't rotate the faceplate.

Following a bearing may bring to you an impassable terrain obstacle, like a cliff. To get around it and return to your original course, you'll basically use the same technique.

First, note the compass bearing of the direction you have to travel to get around the obstacle. As you hike in that direction, count your steps or somehow estimate the distance you're going off-course. Once around the obstacle, reverse the distance you traveled off-course following the bearing opposite the direction you just walked off-course. (If your off-course travel to get around the cliff had been due east, or 90°, you'll reverse the same distance going due west, or 270°.) Once you've recovered the ground you lost going around the terrain obstacle and you're back on your original course, return to following your original bearing to reach your destination.

Following a compass bearing in steep, rugged terrain such as mountains can become challenging. You may have to skirt repeated terrain obstacles or hit a complete dead end in terrain and have to turn around and try another direction. Snow on steep ground adds another, formidable obstacle. It's easy to become disoriented. Make sure your skills at backcountry navigation are well honed before you take off in rough terrain in winter. Observe your surroundings closely; try to remember key natural landmarks.

As you know from your three-season hiking experience, contour lines on a map provide a picture of sorts of the landscape by connecting points that lie at the same elevation. Elevations are marked for some contour lines, in feet or meters. The map legend tells you what the constant interval is between adjacent contour lines, so you can determine the elevation of any point on any contour line. You can figure out the interval by looking at two contour lines whose elevation is marked— usually these lines are bolder than the unmarked lines—and counting the unmarked lines separating them. It's typically four lines, so if the difference in elevation between marked bold lines is 200 feet, then each unmarked line between the bold contours represents a difference up or down of 40 feet in elevation. You can discern uphill and downhill direction by reading the elevations at the marked contour lines and because bends in contour lines point downhill.

Contour lines, of course, provide useful information such as your elevation (precisely or approximately, depending on your nearness to a contour line and the map's level of detail) and the difference in elevation between your current position and your destination. They allow you to "read" the terrain on the map and use that to identify natural features within sight, which can help you figure out your location. They also show the terrain's steepness—lines bunched closely together indicate a steep slope, lines spread out reveal flatter ground—which takes on heightened importance with snow on the ground, both because steep terrain may pose an avalanche hazard (depending on current snow conditions) and because you may want to either avoid or gravitate to steep ground, depending on your skill level on skis or snowshoes. Of course, the ability of contour lines to show detail in the terrain is limited by the contour interval: Any difference in elevation in the terrain that is less than the contour interval will not appear on the map (unless that change happens to occur at a contour interval line).

Global Positioning System

You may never need or choose to use a **Global Positioning System (GPS) receiver** while winter hiking. Some people detest technology in the wilderness; others enjoy using it and see a benefit to it. Nevertheless, don't disregard the usefulness of GPS outright, especially if you intend to get into serious wilderness in winter. A GPS receiver can pinpoint your precise location under many circumstances—something that's hard to do with a simple map and compass when snow obliterates the trail and the landscape around you is ubiquitous, with no features that are readily identifiable on the map. Whether you're winter hiking in the Maine woods, the piney backcountry of Yellowstone National Park, or the remote wilds of Alaska—especially when marked trails disappear under snow cover—a GPS receiver can make the difference between wandering along an approximate course by map and compass not knowing exactly where you are and knowing your precise location. That said, a GPS receiver is of little use unless you know how to apply the information it provides to a map to determine your location.

A GPS receiver picks up signals from U.S. government-operated satellites (originally developed for the Department of Defense) circling 12,000 miles above the Earth's surface. Once a unit gets data from three of the twenty-four satellites, it determines your location and displays it on a liquid crystal display (LCD) screen, either in latitude and longitude or your choice of other coordinate systems. With data from at least four satellites, a GPS receiver can also precisely calculate your altitude.

Many models are multichannel, or parallel-channel, receivers with twelve channels capable of locking onto several satellites simultaneously, establishing your position within seconds (especially after you've recorded a waypoint in the general area) and providing a steady stream of information. They work in most weather conditions, regardless of visibility. They usually function even in dense forests and deep valleys, unless land features prevent your receiver from receiving signals from at least three satellites. Modern GPS receivers can store the coordinates for hundreds (sometimes thousands) of locations, or waypoints, recorded either while you're standing in a particular location (often at the push of a button) or preprogrammed into the unit if you know the coordinates of a location you wish to reach. A command often called "go to" in a GPS receiver literally points you to a waypoint, correcting your direction of travel as you proceed and telling your distance from the destination. You can create and store dozens or hundreds of routes, composed of multiple waypoints, in a receiver. Most units offer numerous functions, including the ability to backtrack a route you've been traveling and to estimate your time of arrival at your destination, a variety of navigational data such as your average speed and distance traveled, and the time of sunrise and sunset in your location. Barometric altimeters, and even the ability to communicate with voice or data between compatible units, are found in the most advanced receivers. Although many GPS receivers cannot tell you whether a cliff or ravine bars your path, increasingly, the technology allows users to download a topographic map into a GPS receiver and read the map on the LCD screen while hiking.

Many GPS receivers weigh less than a pound, fit inside a pocket, and can be operated with one hand. They differ largely in the variety of features they offer and in how they operate: Some may seem more intuitive than others, so it's worth trying out different models before buying. Their weakness is the need for batteries, which drain rapidly, especially in the cold. Look for a model with a battery-saver feature. Long-life, rechargeable lithium batteries cost more but weigh less, last longer, and function longer in the cold than standard alkaline batteries. This technology is evolving rapidly, and prices have come down considerably since GPS receivers first hit the commercial market.

Altimeter

An **altimeter** measures barometric pressure to calculate your altitude above sea level, making it most useful in mountains or any terrain where elevation changes frequently. Knowing your altitude can help you pinpoint your location on the map. An altimeter is a standard piece of gear for mountaineers; but it can be helpful in any snow-covered terrain with constant changes in elevation, where navigation becomes challenging. The shortcoming of an altimeter is that it is affected by changes in barometric pressure, so you have to calibrate it frequently at known elevations (such as trailheads, summits, anyplace where the elevation is marked on the map) to ensure its accuracy—and even then its readings may be suspect or slightly off, making altimeters less precise than GPS receivers.

Because it measures barometric pressure, an altimeter can help forecast weather. If your altimeter's elevation reading goes up when you have not changed altitude—which tends to occur over a period of hours, for instance, while camped overnight—the barometric pressure has dropped, indicating that wet weather is on the way. When an altimeter reading drops despite you not gaining or losing altitude, it indicates a rise in the barometric pressure and improving weather. The altimeter is, however, at best only an approximate forecaster of weather, so continue to use your own judgment in assessing weather changes (see Chapter 5).

Getting "Unlost"

All right, we're grown-ups—we're big enough to admit it: Even the most experienced hikers among us have taken a wrong turn on occasion. We've walked, daydreaming, past a trail junction and not realized our mistake until going well out of our way; or in a moment of uncharacteristic disorientation, we've started off down a trail in the wrong direction. Some of us have even enjoyed the unplanned challenge of discovering we've inadvertently wandered off the trail and suddenly are not quite sure where we are. These things happen. We may not be technically "lost," but we're certainly temporarily misplaced.

In winter, it's a little easier to misplace yourself—snow and downed trees obscure the trail and its markers, the terrain along a familiar trail or route you've taken many times in summer looks completely different in winter, and limited daylight hours sometimes contribute to hikers getting caught out in the woods after dark and finding it harder to follow a trail. Novice winter hikers can be surprised by how easily this happens or even how many times during a single hike.

Wandering aimlessly isn't a great idea in winter: It's fatiguing (especially going off-trail in heavy snow), you may not have enough daytime hours to fritter any away, and it's cold out and sure to get colder as night falls. If you find yourself temporarily misplaced, try some of the following techniques to get back on track.

1. For starters, avoid taking a wrong turn by paying close attention to where you're going. If you realize you've gone astray and there's snow on the ground, retracing your own tracks back to the trail is an easy solution, provided they haven't drifted over.

2. If you don't have tracks to retrace, remain calm—you're probably not far off course. Don't strike off blindly in a direction that "feels right"—that's a good way to get really lost. Look around; find a distinctive landmark like a big tree, clearing, or rock; and remember or mark the spot where you stand in case your first attempt at getting back on course fails and you find yourself back at this point again.

3. Remind yourself which direction you came from and mark it somehow, so that you don't get turned around and completely disoriented, which is remarkably easy to do in a ubiquitous, snow-covered landscape.

4. Are you actually off course? Look around for signs of the trail such as blazes or an obvious trail corridor, including behind you. Sometimes a downed tree will block your view of the trail, making you think you've lost it when in fact you're standing on or near it.

5. If you see no sign of the trail, think about the last time you were certain you were on it and how long ago or how far back that was. Knowing that, you can estimate the maximum distance you could possibly be from the trail. Look at your map and surroundings and try to identify natural features that are within the approximate area you think you are on the map. If you can determine your approximate location, use your map and compass to determine the direction to walk to find your way out.

6. As a last resort, you might try striking off in one direction at a time in search of a place you either know or can identify on the map. Using your compass, first walk in a straight line due north for 10, 20, or 30 minutes, whatever distance seems reasonable. If you find no sign of a trail or anything recognizable to you or identifiable on your map, return to your starting point—the place you first realized you were lost—and walk a similar length of time in a straight line due east. Do the same thing heading south and west, if necessary.

If all of these tactics fail, and you have no idea where you are, remain calm and think out a solution to your predicament. Usually, you'll have two choices:

1. If you're in the mountains in a populous area, walking or following running water downhill will often lead to a road, community, or building where you can get help. However, in a remote area with few roads and communities spread widely apart, this may only get you even more lost. Consult your map before deciding between these options.

2. Wait in the place where you first realized you were off course—as far as you know, it's closer to where you should be than anyplace else nearby. Moreover, by staying put rather than wandering aimlessly, you maximize the odds of searchers finding you at all and minimize the time it will take them to find you. Move to another place only if you can safely get to a spot where you're more visible, like an open meadow.

If you decide to stay put, provide as much help as you can to your searchers. Break branches, tie ribbons, use a mirror or other reflector to signal, write a large-letter message (reading "SOS" or your name) with dark objects like rocks or branches on the snow in a clearing, and/or light a fire in a conspicuous location to signal them. If you change location, leave a note written on paper (put it in a plastic bag or something to keep it dry), with mud on rocks, or with sticks in the dirt or snow, bearing in mind that any message left at ground level could get buried by fresh snowfall. Carry a safety whistle and blow it regularly, in three short blasts. If you see a low-flying plane, lie flat on your back in an open area with your arms outspread and wave your arms; you'll be more visible from the air than if you stood up waving.

Finally, keep in mind that if searchers are looking for you, they'll find you much more quickly if you've left your hiking itinerary, including what time you intended to finish, with someone who'll know whether you've returned from your hike.

Hopefully, you'll have the clothing and gear necessary to survive a cold night outside. If you build an emergency shelter, be sure that searchers can see or locate you from the ground or the air.

Staying Warm and Dry

These four words—*staying warm and dry*—sum up the trick to enjoying winter hiking. Indeed, that theme echoes through the pages of this book. Learn how to achieve those cherished objectives, and you'll revel in the outdoors in winter. Fail at those objectives, and at best, you'll know some measure of misery; at worst, you'll endanger yourself.

Fortunately, the recipe for success builds from one fundamental tenet: Your source of warmth is not your fancy technical clothing—it's your body. The clothing merely insulates and protects your body from the cold and weather—not an insignificant function, to be sure—but it's the heat you generate inside that determines your level of warmth and comfort. Keep this in mind, and the tips laid out later will be easier to remember.

The other basic principle of staying warm in freezing temperatures is to bear in mind that the body parts farthest from your body's heat-producing core—hands and feet, fingers and toes—are naturally the most difficult to keep warm and to warm up if they get cold. Always pay attention to your digits: Do not expose bare hands to extreme cold, especially extreme cold and strong wind; learn to do things while wearing gloves and mittens. When fingers or toes get cold, take action to warm them up again, either by getting your body moving and/or putting on more clothing like a hat, another jacket, or overmitts—or as a last resort, crawling into a sleeping bag and a shelter. An estimated 50 percent of body heat is lost through the top of your head, so wearing a hat can help warm fingers and toes.

As emphasized in Chapter 3, staying properly hydrated and eating enough food are vital to staying warm. When you feel cold, take a drink and eat a snack. Having water and food easily accessible while moving will ensure that you consume both frequently.

Dress appropriately for severe windchill and ice-covered ground.

Movement is the fastest way to warm up, and the more strenuous the activity, the faster you'll generate heat. When you feel chilled, get moving. Walk uphill if one is nearby. Plan snack breaks to be short (and snacks that are quickly ingested), because you'll cool off rapidly and need to get going again within minutes to warm up again.

When you stop for a break, even if for only 5 or 10 minutes, immediately put on a warm jacket and hat. Your body may still cool down quickly, but the extra layers will slow down that cooling process.

Overheating because you've overdressed for your activity level and the ambient temperature and weather conditions is as dangerous as underdressing, because getting your clothing wet with perspiration will cool you down just as quickly as getting soaked in the rain (see Chapter 2). Just as you would immediately add a layer if you felt chilled, if you feel warm, remove a layer. Whenever possible, balance your exertion level and clothing to stay warm without perspiring heavily. For example, if it's snowing, you'll need a jacket that sheds snow, but you may only need a warm shirt underneath it to stay warm while moving.

While on the trail, wear a jacket or pants with pockets you can reach while walking so that you can micro-adjust small clothing items in response to sudden changes in your warmth level—putting on a second pair of gloves or mittens or swapping an earband for a hat, for instance.

Big jacket pockets that are well insulated or lined with mesh allow you to warm hands quickly while on the go. Mesh-lined pockets next to your body's warm core are also the perfect place to dry out wet hand and head wear—these things dry remarkably quickly from body heat as you're moving—and to store hand wear that you're not using at the moment, ensuring that gloves or mittens are warm when you're ready to put them on. One of the quickest ways to make your fingers go numb is to stick them inside cold gloves.

Organize your food, gear, and extra clothing in your pack so that you can quickly get anything you want, to minimize the time you spend standing around cooling down and the time you spend with a warm outer hand layer removed for dexterity. Whereas rummaging around in your pack (or standing around waiting for a companion who's doing that) is merely an annoyance in summer, in winter it can greatly affect your comfort level.

Staying physically fit keeps you warmer, because the metabolism of a fit person generates heat quickly and easily. Fit people are also able to work harder and longer, generating heat.

You can also acclimate your body to freezing temperatures, increasing your tolerance for cold (see Chapter 10).

If you have chronic problems with cold hands and feet, try some of the chemical hand and foot warmer packets available commercially.

Lastly, don't start a hike in freezing temperatures by sticking your feet into cold boots—it'll take forever for your feet to warm up the boots. Before reaching the trailhead, warm your boots up by placing them under your car's heater or tucking them inside your jacket; at the least, don't leave them sitting in a cold trunk.

Hiking Above Tree Line

The alpine terrain above the highest reach of the forest—or tree line—is a sought-after destination for hikers anytime of year. In winter, it transforms into a place of unparalleled beauty—with its attendant challenges. Winter hikers can venture above tree line in any number of mountain ranges in the country, from the Northeast to

Getting above tree line into the alpine zone in winter rewards hikers with beauty and challenge.

the Rockies, Cascades, Sierra Nevada, and Alaska. The alpine zone is best explored with well-developed winter hiking skills; don't treat this inhospitable terrain as a schoolroom for novices.

The ecosystem above tree line is extremely fragile. Although alpine vegetation is not flowering, you can still cause real damage with your boots. Stick to trails when possible, travel atop deep snow, or walk on rocks, sand, and other durable surfaces.

Depending on the terrain's steepness and the presence of snow and ice, you may need an ice ax and crampons to travel safely (see Chapter 2).

Hiking above tree line is complicated most often—and most significantly—by weather. Without the protection of forest, you're completely exposed to wind and precipitation, and as you know, winds tend to be stronger on summits, on ridge tops, and in mountain passes. Winds may be too severe to spend much time above tree line and can be strong enough in some places to lift an adult off the ground or knock one down. You also know that air temperature usually drops as you climb higher, an average of three degrees Fahrenheit for every 1000 feet of altitude but not infrequently more than that. Before heading above tree line, obtain a forecast for the mountains, which is available in some regions. Go fully prepared for severe weather, using many of the skills covered here. In addition, go with the attitude that you may not be able to go farther than tree line on any given day—I've turned back at or just beyond tree line more times than I've gone to a summit above tree line.

Bear in mind that when hiking above tree line on a clear day, you greatly increase your exposure to UV radiation from the sun, especially at elevations above 6000 to 8000 feet and when snow covers the ground, because of the reflective quality of snow. Cover your skin as much as possible and use sunblock (see Chapter 6).

Navigating above tree line can be difficult because the landscape may lack features identifiable on the map, and whiteouts are not uncommon on some high mountains (see Chapter 5). Where you're off-trail or unable to find the trail, maintain a straight line of travel by taking a compass bearing off distant points like rock outcrops or patches of unique vegetation. If the terrain lacks such features, use your map to figure out the compass bearing that will bring you to your destination (see earlier instructions on using map and compass). Depending on where you're going, a GPS receiver can be useful.

Getting Benighted

Spending an unexpected night outside in frigid temperatures, on the frozen ground, is something no winter hiker likes to think about. With smart planning and decision-making, you will, hopefully, never endure such an unenviable event. However, don't assume that experience or even safe, conservative decisions render you immune to bad luck. For a variety of reasons—a sudden storm slowing your progress, an injury late in the day, a party member unprepared for the rigors of the trip—

winter hikers sometimes find themselves inadvertently stranded overnight in the backcountry.

How prepared you should be for an unexpected night outside depends on where you're going, the difficulty of the terrain, and the maximum distance—or more accurately, the maximum time—you'll be from any road and potential help if someone is injured. If you're just out for a short hike in a park or forest with heavily traveled trails, where you won't ever be more than, say, a mile from the nearest road, you probably don't have to carry an emergency sleeping bag—extra clothing should do, just in case you find yourself getting back later than planned. However, if you're day hiking in mountains or a more remote area, potentially some miles from the nearest road, it's imperative that you be ready to survive a winter night outside. Decisions about level of preparedness are certainly subjective, and it's better to err on the side of safety. Part II delves more deeply into winter camping skills that would be helpful for someone who's benighted; this section addresses only how to get through an emergency situation.

Getting benighted typically occurs in one of two ways:

1. A sudden event, like an injury, makes it immediately clear that you will be spending the night outside.
2. A slow progression of events—the party being slowed by weather, trail conditions, fitness level, and/or other factors—leads to you finding yourself in the backcountry after dark falls, forcing you to decide whether to hunker down for the night or try to continue moving in the dark.

Under either scenario, remain calm, so that you'll think more clearly and help your companions stay calm. Remember to continue doing the things necessary to stay warm: Drink and eat enough, and adjust your clothing as needed to avoid cooling down or overheating; it's easy to get distracted by your circumstances and forget these things, which risks worsening your situation. Summon all of your backcountry knowledge and skills to devise a plan to get through the night.

Let's address separately how to deal with the two general scenarios described earlier.

In the first scenario, where an injury or similar event makes it clear you won't avoid getting benighted, you at least avoid wasting time wrestling with the decision about whether to try to keep moving or to hunker down. Instead, you can take immediate steps for your comfort and survival.

Your exertion level will probably drop off as you go from hiking to dealing with a possible emergency, like an injury, and preparing to spend the night outside. The first logical step will likely be to get more clothing on everyone.

Determine whether some members of your party should continue out to the trailhead to summon help for the others. Making this evaluation is essentially the same as the decision-making process laid out under the second scenario, listed earlier and elaborated on later. (See Chapter 6 for how to deal with an injured party.)

To the best of your group's ability (depending on everyone's mobility), find a place that's relatively protected from wind and weather, avoiding sites that are on the lowest ground in the immediate area (because cold air sinks) or that may be exposed to avalanche, falling ice, or other hazards. Considering how long you'll be out there, the effort to move to a better site will be worthwhile.

Divide duties, such as preparing a shelter and melting snow for drinking and cooking water among party members, to keep everyone busy—and thus warm— and to get everything done more quickly.

If you have no shelter like a tent or bivy bag, improvise an emergency shelter with whatever natural materials are available, including snow or sticks and leaves on the ground. An emergency shelter will keep you much warmer than you'd be in the open. It may be as simple as a body-length tunnel dug into a snowbank (which will provide a surprising amount of insulation from the outside cold air) or a wall of snow constructed as a windbreak, or as complex as a snow cave or a structure made of sticks and leaves. To build the latter in an area with little or no snow cover, gather sticks roughly 2 to 3 feet long, or long enough to line up leaning against a downed tree or log and create a space underneath the sticks large enough for a person to lie inside. Pile leaves and any available vegetation (preferably gathered from the ground) atop the sticks, as densely as possible, then add another layer of sticks atop the vegetation to hold it in place. Close off the foot end of the shelter with sticks and vegetation. Building this type of shelter can take time, but the effort will keep you warm, and the shelter could make the difference between staying warm and comfortable or losing digits to frostbite. (See Chapter 10 for instruction in building snow shelters.)

Insulate yourself—and, obviously, any injured companion—from the cold ground with whatever is available: a pack, sleeping pad, climbing rope, or any clothing you're not wearing. Even sitting or lying atop sticks and leaves will cause your body to lose heat more slowly than being in direct contact with snow, ice, or the ground.

If you have no stove for melting snow, look for a source of open water for drinking. Better to take your chances with drinking untreated water than to become dehydrated in freezing temperatures. If all water sources are frozen, pack a small amount of snow into a water bottle and tuck it inside your clothing so your body heat can melt it. (Don't attempt to melt too much snow at once; it will draw precious heat from your body.)

If you're concerned about running out of food before being rescued, ration it sensibly, eating when necessary for warmth or strength.

If you're cold, horde and conserve body heat by sitting balled up and/or huddling with your companions.

Try to provide a signal, such as a fire, to signal rescuers. Rocks in a fire can later be brought into your shelter or sleeping bag; they will give off warmth for some time.

Under the second scenario, in which a slow progression of unexpected delays finds you in the backcountry after dark falls, you may face a difficult subjective decision about whether to hunker down for the night or try to continue moving in the dark back to civilization. Your instinct may be to get out, whatever it takes, rather than spend the night outside; in most cases, that's the wisest course of action. But before deciding to continue through the darkness, ask yourself these questions:

▲ Do you have reliable light sources that will last as long as it will take to get out?
▲ Is the weather so severe, or could a building storm become so severe, that it would be safer to find a protected place to spend the night rather than continuing in darkness?
▲ Does everyone in the party have the energy to continue, or will going on risk an injury that could abruptly change your situation from not good to serious?
▲ Is everyone emotionally comfortable with continuing?
▲ Could darkness make following your intended route difficult or impossible? If so, is there a preferable alternate escape route to take in the dark?
▲ Will you face any unavoidable obstacles, like a water crossing, that could be too dangerous to consider attempting in the dark?
▲ Is there a reasonable expectation that you can get out before daylight? Are the remaining distance and your likely speed of travel such that you'd probably spend hours moving in the dark and might get out faster and safer by simply waiting for first light before going on?

If you decide to keep moving rather than prepare a rough campsite for the night, remember the following:

▲ Continue eating and drinking sufficiently to maintain your energy level and to stay warm.
▲ Darkness magnifies distances in our minds and distorts our sense of time. Pay attention to the time and your map and have some sense of your speed to determine how far you've gone and where you are.
▲ Move slowly, watching the ground ahead to avoid falling. Changes in the terrain can be difficult to see when snow covers everything and you're following the beam of a headlamp—you can suddenly find yourself tipping off an embankment into a snow-covered creek bed. If you have a second light, try carrying it so that its beam strikes the ground at a different angle than your angle of vision to the ground (for example, carrying it in your hand).
▲ If you're concerned about your light's batteries dying, conserve power by having only every other member in the party using a light at any time or traveling only by moonlight if it's bright enough. Don't forgo using a light if the terrain and poor lighting present a risk of injury. You might also revive cold batteries by sticking them in a warm pocket next to your body for a while.

- Make conservative decisions. Everything becomes more dangerous in the dark, from stream and creek crossings to moving over slippery or rugged ground.
- Go with the thought in mind that you can still hunker down for the night if you deem at any point that continuing is unsafe.

Similarly, before deciding to spend an unplanned night outside rather than continuing after dark, consider these questions:
- Is everyone emotionally comfortable with spending a winter night outside?
- Do you all have the gear and clothing to get through a night in subfreezing temperatures and potentially bad weather?
- Is anyone's physical condition so precarious—perhaps because of injury or advancing hypothermia—that it would be unwise to try to survive a night outside?
- Can you find a protected place to spend the night?

If you decide to spend the night outside, follow the guidelines listed earlier under the first emergency scenario.

When out on a day hike, even if prepared to survive getting benighted, there's a significant psychological threshold to cross in deciding to hunker down for a night outside in winter. It may be wiser to stay put in a good, if improvised, shelter rather than to continue in darkness and potentially severe weather, with party members growing more exhausted. Weigh your level of preparedness to spend the night against your readiness and ability to get out in the dark. If your biggest concern is staying warm, and party members are feeling good, maintaining a slow but steady pace while continuing to the trailhead can be the best way to keep everyone warm and safe.

Going Solo

Hiking alone in winter may be the last thing you'd attempt, and if so, that's well and good. The old maxim against hiking alone is embraced by many three-season hikers and only becomes more relevant in winter. Without question, going solo in wintry conditions greatly increases your risk level: Should anything happen to you that limits or impedes your mobility, no one will even know you may be in trouble until some time after you were scheduled to return from your hike, meaning a search for you won't begin until potentially hours after your injury—and possibly not until the next day. This presumes, of course, that you've notified a responsible person of when you expected to get back from the hike (a good idea). Should you suffer an injury while alone that leaves you unconscious or unable to improvise shelter or get into extra clothing—and this could happen in any number of ways in temperatures around or below freezing—you could well suffer severe, irreversible frostbite or die of hypothermia before anyone finds you. Don't underestimate the risks of hiking solo in winter.

That said, it would be irresponsible to not acknowledge that some experienced winter hikers will venture out solo. I've done it numerous times, and although I wouldn't recommend it for an inexperienced winter hiker, I wouldn't recommend *against* it for a hiker who is adequately experienced and prepared. It can be a challenging and rewarding way to expand on your winter hiking experiences. If you decide to take up solo hiking in winter conditions, follow these guidelines:

▲ Give your itinerary to someone who will know if you do not return on schedule, and stick to your plan—or any alternate escape route spelled out in your itinerary—so that searchers know where to look for you.

▲ Don't overestimate your abilities, experience, or current fitness level. Always be honest with yourself, remembering that having done a particular solo hike in the past does not automatically ensure you are ready to do it today.

▲ Make sure you know the environment you're entering well and its hazards and challenges. I'm not saying you should only hike solo in places you've already gone previously in a group; nor am I suggesting that having gone someplace

Sharing the Backcountry with Other Users

Winter invites different types of recreational activities in the backcountry and people with different ideas of how to have fun. Sometimes the places where these different groups seek out their own style of adventure overlap. When this happens, and different groups fail to respect the others' equal right to be there, conflict can arise.

In winter as in other seasons, the conflict typically occurs between nonmotorized users—hikers, skiers, and snowshoers—and motorized users (that is, people on snowmobiles or, where the ground remains bare in winter, all-terrain vehicles). In many places where skiers and snowshoers have found the number and behavior of snowmobilers to be an intrusion on their backcountry experience (the nature of the two modes of travel rarely creates a situation where snowmobilers are irked by the presence of skiers or snowshoers), opposing interests, in concert with the land manager, have been able to work out mutually agreeable designated zones for motorized and nonmotorized activity—separating the groups for everyone's benefit. It's a tactic that produces much better results than grumbling or exchanging hostile words.

If you'd rather not encounter motorized users when in the backcountry, research your destination and find out whether, and where, motors are permitted and prohibited. Similarly, if you use a snowmobile to access deeper backcountry—as snowshoers and skiers do in some regions of the country—be aware of regulations governing where machines are permitted and prohibited, and follow them. For instance, you can often use machines to travel on snow-covered national forest roads but must park the machines outside the boundary of designated wilderness areas and proceed on foot from there. State and other lands have their own rules.

◀ Only experienced hikers should head out solo in winter, especially above tree line.

previously with a group is, by itself, adequate training for doing the same hike alone in winter. You should have a thorough enough knowledge of your destination, through researching it or prior experience in similar circumstances, that nothing you could encounter will surprise you. Venturing into the unknown can be a formula for disaster in winter.

▲ Recognize that pushing yourself to the extremes of your abilities and stamina when going solo puts you at much more significant risk, especially in winter, than a solo outing well below your ability level.

▲ Recognize also that striking out solo in a remote area not frequented by people in winter may greatly reduce the likelihood of getting help should you need it.

▲ Make conservative decisions when you're alone, always weighing the possibility and consequences of your actions.

▲ Keep in mind that no matter how excited you may be about a particular challenging objective, nothing is more important than getting back home safely.

Children and Winter

There's no reason that children of all ages can't enjoy winter in the outdoors as much as adults, provided the adults responsible for them don't lose sight of a child's limits. A snow-covered landscape provides a natural playground for young children—they will have fun. You'll find some of these tips applicable in any season, but they ring even more true in winter.

▲ With infants and preschool-aged children, the greatest challenges are keeping them warm and the physical limits on how fast and far they can go under their own power in snow. Child-carrier sleds, especially models that can be closed up to shield their occupants from wind and weather, keep a baby or tot much warmer than carrying the child in a pack. A sled provides shelter and space for blankets and insulating pads under the child, whereas a child in a pack has only his or her own clothing for protection from the elements, and a pack's cockpit compresses clothing, inhibiting its ability to insulate the child. Arrange a child in a sled so that he or she can sleep comfortably, using blankets or clothing as pillows and padding.

▲ Hang a few small toys from a child-carrier pack, or put the toys in the sled with a child.

▲ Set reasonable goals for children, understanding that moving on snow can quickly exhaust them, especially young kids. Encourage them to move under their own power, but be prepared to carry young ones when they get tired. Increase distance and difficulty gradually; few things will discourage young adventurers faster than pushing them too far.

▲ Involve children of all ages in the planning and execution of the hike—letting them help select the destination and giving them age-appropriate duties on the trail. Giving them ownership in the adventure enhances their enthusiasm for it.

Children can enjoy the backcountry in winter.

▲ Children of all ages (beyond young toddlers) enjoy having peers along—and it reduces the amount of complaining they do. Let them invite friends.

▲ Especially with young children, bring a comfort item such as their favorite stuffed animal.

▲ Invent games to play along the trail, involving things in the surrounding environment, to entertain young children; or simply encourage them to lead the hike and "scout" the trail.

▲ Children both overheat faster than adults (their body's natural cooling system is not developed) and get cold faster than adults (children have a higher ratio of body surface area to body mass than an adult, which speeds the loss of core body heat). When the temperature drops or the wind kicks up, get extra clothing on kids right away—they'll need it sooner and you'll feel the need for it. Create opportunities for them to drink and snack more frequently than adults, and bring food they'll want to eat.

▲ Children tend to get hats and mittens wet; carry extra ones.

▲ Monitor a child's hands, ears, nose, and feet to make sure they're warm. With the first three, it's easy to do even with a sleeping child. The only reason to be concerned about a child's feet is if his or her boots are inadequate or get wet, or obviously, if the child complains about cold feet or appears uncomfortable. Look for children's mittens with a zipper, for ease getting them on and a more snug fit to ensure they stay on.

▲ A child's skin is more sensitive to sunburn than an adult's and more susceptible to long-term damage by overexposure to sun. Use clothing and children's sunblock (reapplying the latter frequently) to protect their skin.

▲ Outfit your child with the same quality of outdoor clothing and gear as you demand—as it does with you, being warm and comfortable will make a big difference in your child's enjoyment.

Smile Through Your Tears

Sure, it sounds silly and may strike you as annoying and ill-timed advice should you hear someone utter those four words during a particularly difficult moment in the backcountry. However, this advice is intended as seriously as anything else in this book. We simply cannot strike off into the backcountry in winter—or winterlike conditions—and expect everything to go well, or react angrily or irrationally when it doesn't. Things have an amazing way of going wrong in winter, even more so than in the warmer months. Letting anger and frustration get the best of you not only makes your company less pleasant but also can create panic or irrational reactions among your companions and get in the way of dealing appropriately with an emergency or potentially serious situation. Maintaining a sense of humor and a positive attitude is your best weapon against the unexpected.

Chapter 5

Weather

inter hiking" takes on different meanings depending on where in the country you hike. In many mountain areas, "winter"—or weather conditions that many hikers would describe as wintry—commences by mid- or late autumn and continues well into spring. At higher elevations in mountain ranges from the Northeast to the West and Alaska, snow can fall in any month of the year, and nighttime low temperatures can dip below freezing even in summertime. While anyone familiar with conditions during the calendar months of winter in places like the northern Rockies or New Hampshire's Presidential Range wouldn't equate true winter with the occasional summer snow squall, the weather knowledge in this chapter is relevant virtually year-round.

Weather and Decision-Making

The fact that you're reading this book suggests that you're willing to tolerate colder temperatures and perhaps a modest mix of meteorological madness. The weather is a big part of the adventure, after all. Underestimating the potential severity of a winter storm has invited a mess of hurt on many a winter hiker. Even on a clear day, severe cold and wind may turn you around faster than a freezing rain. Beyond the basic question of your preparedness for a winter hike, the variable most likely to influence your decisions on the trail—or even at the trailhead—is the weather. The following should always factor into your decision-making process when hiking in winter:

▲ Check the forecast before your hike, looking for a forecast specific to your backcountry destination rather than the nearest city or town, which might receive different weather.

▲ Monitor closely any changes in the weather during the day, especially when you're above tree line.

▲ Be aware of all potential escape routes and places where you might find some shelter from the weather.

▲ Communicate with your companions—make sure everyone is comfortable with the group's plan.

▲ Most importantly: Don't be excessively goal oriented. Always embark on a winter adventure with the conscious understanding (among everyone in your party) that weather could force you to change your plans. Going out focused myopically on your objective can cloud your judgment and delay your recognition of when it's time to abandon Plan A and resort to Plan B.

Weather Information Resources

Checking the day's weather forecast should be as routine a part of your preparation for a winter hike as lacing up your boots. Most importantly, seek out a forecast specific to your backcountry destination—its weather will often be different than the weather in the nearest metropolitan area, which is the forecast you'll hear on most TV and radio stations headquartered in cities. Pay attention to the forecast a couple of days in advance of your hike—it's helpful to know, for instance, whether significant snowfall has accumulated where you'll be hiking before your arrival—but understand that the accuracy of forecasts drops off dramatically when looking ahead more than 24 hours.

TV news or weather channels can be reliable when providing a forecast specific to your destination, rather than for the nearest city, which may experience different weather.

Commercial, public, or weather radio, as with TV stations, are useful when providing a forecast specific to your destination; weather radio is typically the best source, and it's widely available.

The current day's newspaper will have some information about the forecast, but bear in mind that it's probably at least 12 hours old.

The World Wide Web is a timely resource; try the National Weather Service website (http://weather.noaa.gov/weather/ccus.html) or the site of a commercial weather channel or area weather observatory.

Land-management agencies and regional hiking groups sometimes post the day's forecast outside a ranger station, visitor center, or office, or have a recorded daily forecast available at their phone number.

Lastly, make a habit of asking people in a local store or other hikers in the trailhead parking lot what they've heard for a forecast and what they know about the recent weather and conditions in the backcountry. Local knowledge is sometimes your best source of accurate and timely information.

Talk weather with someone who has logged many trail days winter hiking in one region, and you may hear that person talk more about the area's regional climate than that day's forecast. Experienced hikers know these things for a reason: Many regions, especially anyplace with significant variations in elevation or a major water body nearby, exhibit weather patterns that vary seasonally but are frequently consistent from, say, one winter to the next winter. For instance, the bulk of a winter's snowfall may usually occur early in the season. The area may be prone to long spells of clear, dry, cold days, or frequent, dramatic changes in weather from one day to the next. It may commonly see early-winter inversions, where the coldest air pools in the valleys and warmer air rises, so that the temperature goes up as you gain altitude rather than the other way around. The western slopes of high mountains in the West often receive more precipitation than the eastern slopes, but this is not so for the Appalachian Mountains, which get hit from both sides. Coastal areas typically receive wet, heavy snow, whereas inland areas receive much drier, powdery snow. The wind may come prevailingly from one direction, affecting everything from your exposure to the wind to where on the landscape the bulk of snowfall gets deposited. Daily high and low temperatures may show huge swings or remain consistently within a narrow range.

The point is this: Knowing regional climate and weather patterns can be as useful as knowing that day's forecast. Do your research on an area and once you become familiar with it, you'll find yourself almost instinctively anticipating changes in weather and making smarter decisions about where to go, and when.

Reading the Sky

Beyond learning the day's forecast and knowing regional climate and weather patterns, once on the trail you have only your own eyes and brain to rely on in evaluating changes in the weather. The forecast is important, but sometimes it's wrong, or the corner of the backcountry where you find yourself will receive some localized weather that's different from the weather just over the ridge. Keep an eye on the sky, talk about any changes in the weather that appear to be taking place during the day, so that everyone's thinking about it, and learn how to recognize common types of clouds and what they signal, including the following:

High, wispy cirrus clouds, called "mare's tails," herald the arrival of rain or snow within 24 hours.

When a *lenticular cloud*—also known as a "cap" cloud for its resemblance to a giant bowl suspended upside-down above a peak—forms above a mountain, you can be sure its upper elevations are getting hammered by strong winds. It also means precipitation is likely to follow within 48 hours.

Puffy, white cumulus clouds may bring nothing more than wind. Yet if they thicken, or form a solid overcast, precipitation may soon follow.

Low, fast-moving, or "scudding," clouds are usually accompanied by strong wind

Lenticular clouds are wavelike in appearance and often suggest precipitation within 48 hours. (From Cox, Steven M., and Kris Fulsaas, eds. *Mountaineering: The Freedom of the Hills.* 7th ed. Seattle: The Mountaineers Books, 2003.)

With continued upward growth, cumulus clouds suggest showers later in the day.

A halo is commonly seen 24 to 48 hours before precipitation.

and may signal a coming change—a storm surrendering to clear skies, or conversely, an advancing storm.

A reliable old weather gauge used by mariners, farmers, and others for centuries is observing rings formed around the sun or moon: A wide ring, or **halo,** usually means precipitation will begin within 24 to 48 hours; a tight ring, or **corona,** signals precipitation coming within 12 to 24 hours.

What's That Thermometer Say?

One of the greatest challenges of winter is the huge range of temperatures that are possible during the cold months, from above freezing to far below zero. Winter hiking novices don't always immediately comprehend the vastness of that range—after all, cold is cold, right? Wrong. Although normal winter temperature range varies with regional climate and latitude, many U.S. mountain ranges can see temperatures from thirty degrees above to thirty degrees or forty degrees below Fahrenheit during winter. That's roughly the same as the difference between twenty-five degrees and ninety-five degrees Fahrenheit, and you will feel the difference between cold and extremely cold just as much as you'll feel the difference between hot and cold.

The challenges you'll face and how you react to them are largely dictated by temperature. Temperature can affect the ground surface you're traveling on; your speed, agility, and mobility (by how much clothing you have to wear, what's on your feet, and ground surface conditions); your physical and emotional comfort level; the ease with which you can consume (and procure) water without it freezing; your hand and finger dexterity and the difficulty of performing simple tasks;

the relative threat of frostbite to extremities and exposed skin; and, of course, your plans.

Everyone has a different tolerance for cold, so several people may all "feel" the same temperature and weather conditions differently. Perception of "cold" is subjective. I've distilled some objective observations about how different temperatures affect the winter adventurer and drawn some subjective conclusions that may be helpful in a general way for anyone heading out in winter. Using the Fahrenheit scale, I've outlined what one can generally expect in the wide range of temperatures possible in winter in many U.S. mid-latitude locales. These descriptions refer only to ambient air temperatures, not taking into account the added effect of wind.

Above Freezing

In many ways, life gets more difficult for the winter hiker when the thermometer rises into the mid- and high thirties. First, nothing remains frozen, so you can get wet from what's underfoot (slogging or postholing through wet, slushy snow or muddy trail), from snow and ice melting and dripping out of trees overhead or on trailside vegetation, and from precipitation—instead of dry snow sliding cleanly off your shell, you're getting rain, sleet, or something similarly sloppy. Wet clothing increases your body's heat loss through conduction by a factor of as much as twenty-five, so thirty-five degrees in wet weather can feel colder than twenty-five degrees in dry weather. A melting snow surface underfoot may also cause wet snow to ball up under a snowshoe cleat or crampon or stick to the underside of skis (and climbing skins), making travel slow, aggravating, and potentially hazardous. Although temperatures in the thirties won't feel warm when you're standing around, while you're moving, especially going uphill in humid conditions or precipitation, it's hard to avoid working up a sweat and getting your base layers wet. Making the right clothing choices in these conditions can be a challenge. That said, it could certainly be pleasant to hike in temperatures above freezing on a dry, sunny day.

Mid-Twenties to Thirty-Two Degrees

Things get easier once the temperature slips below freezing—primarily because water in the environment is less troublesome in its frozen state than thawed. Many of the problems described in the previous paragraph are eliminated, meaning your clothing and gear, including the footgear in contact with the frozen ground surface, all stays dry. Many people find this a comfortable range to be moving outside—in fact, it can still be easy to overheat, so be careful not to overdress (shirtsleeves may be all you need). In temperatures just below freezing, though, precipitation is likely to come in the form of wet snow, which can get clothing wet and create problems with footgear on wet snow.

The Teens to Low Twenties

In many respects, this is the ideal temperature range for winter outdoor recreation. The environment is solidly frozen and dry, the air at a temperature that allows you to work hard without easily overheating (though you still have to pay attention to dressing smartly), and any precipitation will come as a nice, dry snow that slides off shell clothing and makes for smooth foot travel. Still, it's not so cold that you can't stop for long without beginning to shiver even with all of your extra clothing. Clear, windless days at this temperature are blessings to be cherished.

Zero Degrees to Ten Degrees

Being outdoors begins to grow more challenging when the thermometer slips down into single digits. Whereas the environment remains thankfully frozen, our bodies have a more difficult time in this kind of cold. Exposed skin, especially extremities, can go numb quickly and be hard to warm. The need to wear gloves and/or mittens virtually at all times hinders dexterity, complicating manual tasks, and if there's much wind you may have to cover your face to guard against frostbite. It's harder to keep feet warm. If you don't take precautions to prevent it, your water bottle cap and contents may freeze, as can many food items. Rest breaks necessarily become brief and demand that you put on all extra clothing to avoid getting chilled quickly. Any emergency automatically becomes more serious.

The Teens Below Zero to Zero Degrees

This enters the realm of "severe cold." Everything described in the previous paragraph gets multiplied. A bottle of water can freeze solid remarkably quickly; you have to perform tasks with heavy hand wear on at all times and pay close attention to body parts at particular risk of frostbite. Unless you're going to set up a full campsite, you'll need to keep moving almost constantly to maintain warmth.

Below Roughly Twenty Degrees Below Zero

Brrrrr. This is extreme and holds a high potential danger. Take everything you've read in the two previous paragraphs and ratchet it up several notches on the scale of difficulty. You'll have to call upon all your cold-weather skills, always working from that fundamental tenet of winter hiking—that your body is your only source of heat (see Chapter 4)—and using physical exertion to keep yourself warm. Although it's certainly possible to go out in these temperatures, don't mess around in such conditions without plenty of prior experience in below-zero temperatures. Moreover, if you can expect much wind, it's probably best to stay home.

One note of advice: Carry a thermometer. You can pick up a small one cheaply; even models that record the maximum and minimum temperatures of the previous 24 hours are relatively inexpensive. A thermometer can be a valuable tool—and not just for boasting to family and friends later about how cold it was. Checking a

Low ambient temperatures and strong winds require proper clothing and footwear.

thermometer routinely can tip you off to a gradual rise or drop in the temperature before you might notice it yourself. A thermometer is also a more accurate gauge of the ambient temperature than your body, and if you feel yourself growing colder but can confirm that the temperature hasn't actually dropped, or dropped much, that's a good signal that you need not only more clothing but some fuel (food and water) to stoke your internal furnace. Knowing the ambient temperature, or seeing a measurable trend up or down in the temperature, may help you make better-informed decisions.

Wind

Without question, wind combined with cold temperatures is a marriage of harsh elements that can make your hike uncomfortable or even downright dangerous. Wind causes the loss of body heat through convection; in warm temperatures, we want to lose body heat, but in winter we do not. As you know, we prevent convectional heat loss to wind by donning windproof shell garments. However, extreme cold and strong winds can still rob you of valuable body heat even when wearing windproof shells. The breathability of shells becomes important in strong winds, too—you have to be able to close up your shell against the wind without overheating while exerting. Whereas wind is rarely a factor in decision-making in summer—unless, say, you're on a narrow, exposed mountain ridge—in winter it can frequently be a reason to alter or abandon your plans.

Seasoned hikers are familiar with the term **windchill.** Many have seen the chart known as the Windchill Temperature Index (Illustration 5-1), used by the National Weather Service, that for decades has provided a measure of the effective temperature—or equivalent temperature, if you will—of a range of ambient air temperatures and wind speeds. The index was simply a way of putting a number on a reality many of us already knew: When it's cold outside, wind always makes it feel colder, and the stronger the wind, the colder it feels. The chart long in use was based on data from 1945.

In 2000 several U.S. and Canadian federal agencies, academic researchers, and the International Society of Biometeorology formed a group whose goal was to evaluate and improve the windchill formula and standardize the Windchill Index internationally, using modern science, technology, and computer modeling. The new windchill index, now in use in the United States and Canada, is considered more accurate than the previous chart, and the windchill temperatures it gives over much of the chart's range (from forty degrees to thirty-five degrees below Fahrenheit and winds of 3 to 60 mph) are less severe than the original chart calculated. For example, with an air temperature of five degrees Fahrenheit and a wind speed of 25

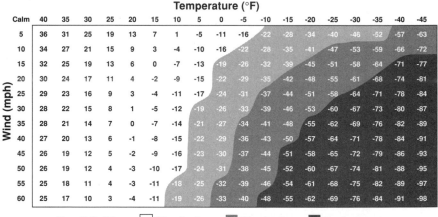

Temperature (°F)

Calm	40	35	30	25	20	15	10	5	0	-5	-10	-15	-20	-25	-30	-35	-40	-45
5	36	31	25	19	13	7	1	-5	-11	-16	-22	-28	-34	-40	-46	-52	-57	-63
10	34	27	21	15	9	3	-4	-10	-16	-22	-28	-35	-41	-47	-53	-59	-66	-72
15	32	25	19	13	6	0	-7	-13	-19	-26	-32	-39	-45	-51	-58	-64	-71	-77
20	30	24	17	11	4	-2	-9	-15	-22	-29	-35	-42	-48	-55	-61	-68	-74	-81
25	29	23	16	9	3	-4	-11	-17	-24	-31	-37	-44	-51	-58	-64	-71	-78	-84
30	28	22	15	8	1	-5	-12	-19	-26	-33	-39	-46	-53	-60	-67	-73	-80	-87
35	28	21	14	7	0	-7	-14	-21	-27	-34	-41	-48	-55	-62	-69	-76	-82	-89
40	27	20	13	6	-1	-8	-15	-22	-29	-36	-43	-50	-57	-64	-71	-78	-84	-91
45	26	19	12	5	-2	-9	-16	-23	-30	-37	-44	-51	-58	-65	-72	-79	-86	-93
50	26	19	12	4	-3	-10	-17	-24	-31	-38	-45	-52	-60	-67	-74	-81	-88	-95
55	25	18	11	4	-3	-11	-18	-25	-32	-39	-46	-54	-61	-68	-75	-82	-89	-97
60	25	17	10	3	-4	-11	-19	-26	-33	-40	-48	-55	-62	-69	-76	-84	-91	-98

(Wind (mph) — row labels)

Frostbite Times ☐ 30 minutes ■ 10 minutes ■ 5 minutes

Windchill (°F) = 35.74 + 0.6215T - 35.75($V^{0.16}$) + 0.4275T($V^{0.16}$)

Where T = Air Temperature (°F) and V = Wind Speed (mph)

Illustration 5-1: A modern windchill chart shows the effective temperature of various combinations of wind speed and ambient air temperature. (From Cox, Steven M., and Kris Fulsaas, eds. *Mountaineering: The Freedom of the Hills.* 7th ed. Seattle: The Mountaineers Books, 2003.)

Wear a face mask to protect your skin from frostbite in severe windchill.

mph, the old chart put windchill temperature at thirty-seven degrees below Fahrenheit, whereas the new chart puts it at seventeen degrees below Fahrenheit. The new chart also provides a calculation of how fast frostbite can occur in exposed skin at windchill temperatures across the chart. You can view the chart, and calculate windchill, at *www.nws.noaa.gov/om/windchill/*.

Studying this chart is prudent schooling for the winter hiker: It gives you a basic sense of where you start getting into the danger zone with wind and cold. Knowing the day's weather forecast for temperatures and wind, and glancing at the chart, gives you a good idea of how severe it may be before you even leave home.

Beyond windchill, the other important thing to bear in mind about wind is that it can be remarkably consistent both in its direction (within a particular area or region) and in where and when it shows up. Two factors contribute to the consistent patterns of wind: prevailing wind direction and orographic effect. The first is self-explanatory—in many areas, the wind frequently comes from the same direction. The term **orographic effect** refers to wind coming up against a mountain or ridge, forcing the wind to flow up and over the land. This essentially funnels a lot of wind through the first break in the landscape it encounters, such as a pass or gap, or up over the summit. This is why the wind at mountain passes and summits, and along the crest of a ridge, is often as much as twice as strong as winds even a short distance below the summit, pass, or ridge.

Know the prevailing wind direction where you are hiking, and you can look at a topographic map and anticipate where you'll encounter the strongest winds along your hiking route—the passes, summits, and ridge crests as well as the windward slopes and the high plateaus in the lee of gaps. The amount of wind predicted in the day's forecast refers to wind speed in the general area—not wind speed in places where topography concentrates the wind—but it gives you some idea of what to expect in areas of heavy wind. This information can help you decide where to hike as well as to anticipate the clothing adjustments you'll need to guard against that wind.

Storms

All of the water in the Earth's oceans, atmosphere, underground, and frozen in ice adds up to about 326 million cubic miles of water, the U.S. Geological Survey estimates. A fraction of that, only about 3100 cubic miles of water, is in the air at any time as water vapor (mostly), clouds, or precipitation. Still, that's a lot of buckets of water.

Winter storms can bring precipitation in many forms, some of them rather unpleasant. A book such as this would not be complete without a short tutorial on the various personalities of inclement weather one can encounter.

We'll start with a basic overview of weather systems. *Air pressure* is the weight of the atmosphere pressing down on the earth (measured by a barometer in units called *millibars*). In calm weather, the barometer rarely drops much below thirty. A high-pressure system usually brings cooler temperatures and clear skies. A low-pressure system brings the opposite: warmer temperatures, storms, and rain. Air pressure decreases as you gain altitude because there are fewer air molecules over-head. A barometric altimeter, which measures barometric pressure to calculate altitude, can help forecast weather (see Chapter 4).

Snow is generally the preferred form of precipitation in winter. We've all seen wet snow and dry snow; in fact, the water content of snow, or amount of water per square inch of snow, can vary greatly. Dry snow may hold as little as around 5 percent water—meaning that every 10 inches of snow will produce, when melted, a half-inch of water. Wet snow might be around 20 to 25 percent water. Snow falling at temperatures near freezing can weigh three times as much as snow falling at colder temperatures, simply because it has a much higher water content. Air at warmer temperatures just below freezing can hold more moisture than colder air.

Wet snow not only gets your shell clothing wet but can complicate traveling on skis, snowshoes, or crampons. In the relatively warm temperatures at which wet snow falls, it is also difficult to keep from overheating underneath your shell when you're exerting. Dry snow is generally ideal for traveling on skis or snow-shoes; but when a lot of it falls quickly, it can be so deep and fluffy that your skis or snowshoes will sink in deeply, making movement strenuous and slow. After a heavy snowfall of light powder, it may take a day or two for the snow to consolidate enough to keep you afloat on skis or snowshoes. Coastal areas near oceans typically receive wet, heavy snow, and inland areas receive much drier, powdery snow. Early-season snowfall in many regions—both coastal and inland—often tends to be wet.

Freezing rain is rain that freezes on contact with a surface that is cooler than the rain's freezing temperature. It's cold, wet, and makes the ground a treacherous skating rink—in a word, ugly.

Sleet, or *ice pellets,* consists specifically of frozen raindrops or refrozen melted snowflakes that are about 0.3 inches—or 7.6 millimeters—or less in diameter. The shape of the ice pellets may be spherical or irregular, and they can be either translucent or transparent. Whereas freezing rain turns the ground into a skating rink, sleet is one notch lower on the miserable and treacherous scale, covering the ground with tiny ball bearings of ice but not as wet as freezing rain.

Although *cold rain* isn't a term you'll encounter in meteorology, it bears mentioning as a form of winter precipitation. Still, many winter hikers, especially in

Hikers at Mount Washington, New Hampshire, descend in a whiteout.

coastal areas, will encounter rain falling at temperatures just above freezing. I recall one day in New Hampshire's White Mountains when an overnight snowfall changed to a torrential rain as the morning brought warmer temperatures. Two friends and I hiked for hours through the deluge, on a trail where an inch of water overlay a crust of ice that we punched through with every third or fourth step, sinking knee-deep into slushy, waterlogged snow beneath the ice. This kind of weather may be the ugliest of the ugly: cold, wet, and decidedly miserable.

Freezing fog is a term used in some mountain ranges to describe just what the name implies—foggy conditions that put a layer of ice on surfaces without precipitation actually occurring. The technical term for the phase change of water vapor in the air directly into ice—or, vice versa, the conversion of ice directly into water vapor—is *sublimation.*

The term **whiteout** describes snowfall so heavy, or a fog so dense, that the milky color of the air blends seamlessly into the equally milky and featureless snow-covered ground. It occurs in terrain lacking trees or other vegetation. It's disorienting to not be able to distinguish the ground and can be dangerous because it may be impossible to see a sudden drop-off in front of you or to find your way (expert map and compass skills are required). If possible, hunker down and wait it out. If you must go on, determine the direction you should be moving and take and follow a compass bearing (see Chapter 4).

Chapter 6

Backcountry Ailments

O n the scale of relative risk to life and limb, hiking ranks pretty low among all the activities undertaken by people outdoors. Despite the occasional dark warnings about backcountry hazards offered in this book, hiking—even in winter—produces few accidents and injuries. A close look at accident reports from U.S. national parks shows that many incidents that result in injury, or require the assistance of park personnel, often involve people who were ill-prepared for even a short, warm-weather hike—who were, one might surmise, inexperienced hikers. Winter hikers tend to be people with a respectable hiking resume, who know enough to avoid the type of problems and accidents that are easily avoidable (which is why I emphasize winter hiking's hazards—knowledge is freedom). Anyone reading this has amassed some knowledge about staying safe in the backcountry before even opening this book.

Still, accidents happen, and as much as we prefer to think otherwise, they sometimes happen to smart, experienced people. There's a great danger in starting to believe that, because we're experienced, nothing bad can happen to us; that attitude breeds complacency. Talk to an experienced hiker, climber, or backcountry skier who has been in a serious accident, and often that person will say, "You know, at the time, I didn't think there was anything to worry about, and I probably wasn't paying attention like I should have been."

Your decisions about how to handle a backcountry injury are of necessity different in winter than in summer. Foremost, though, winter hikers have to become expert at avoiding accidents and injuries, including the most seemingly minor injuries, like blisters. This chapter discusses how to avoid and deal with a variety of ailments most relevant to the winter environment.

Blisters

Blisters form because the outer layers of your foot's skin can move more than the sensitive inner layers can, and the pressure and friction applied by boots and socks as you walk sometimes causes skin layers to separate. Fluid fills the void and, voila, a blister. A foot that's warm and damp inside a boot is more susceptible to getting a blister. Blisters can be painful and slow you down or stop you—if you'll pardon the winter pun—cold.

You don't want to expose your bare foot to freezing temperatures, especially if any precipitation is falling or the wind is blowing—frostbite is much more serious than a blister. Thus, blister avoidance takes on paramount importance in winter.

Foot Care and Customized Footbeds

Injure your hand, arm, shoulder, clavicle, or even crack a rib in the backcountry, and you can probably still walk out to civilization under your own power. But hurt a foot—even something as seemingly mundane as a blister—and you might be waiting for a ride in a gurney. Good, preventive foot care helps keep you out of trouble. Consider the following tips.

▲ In winter, your feet will spend hours inside big, warm boots. Keep them dry. If your feet tend to sweat a lot, use a roll-on antiperspirant on the bottom of your feet, or an antifungal powder on your feet and in your socks and shoes, before and after a hike.

▲ Don't wear boots that are severely worn, are not broken in, or cause you pain.

▲ If you have recurring foot problems (or any injury), don't ignore them. See a doctor—preferably, a doctor with experience treating athletic injuries. It won't just go away.

▲ Many boots come with flimsy foam inserts that add a little cushioning but do nothing to stabilize your foot or reduce motion inside the boot. Customized footbeds, or orthotics, sold over the counter, are simply inserts that provide more support than factory inserts. Good footbeds—ones with a rigid shank to absorb all the stress of bearing weight—are beneficial for many people, can alleviate many sources of foot pain, and are inexpensive. They can improve fit, comfort, and structural stability of any boot, plus prevent foot elongation, blisters, calluses, and other short- and long-term problems.

▲ If you have foot problems that persist after trying over-the-counter inserts, see a podiatrist about getting a truly customized insert designed for your foot.

To prevent cold-related problems in winter, wear the right clothing, especially on your hands and feet. ▶

Make sure your boots fit properly; waterproof-breathable (W-B) models keep wetness out and help prevent your feet from overheating. Wear clean, dry socks (carry a second pair to change into if your feet perspire heavily and you expect to have an opportunity to change socks during your hike), and gaiters or pants that keep snow and water out of your boots. If you anticipate any problem spots on your feet, prep them in the warmth of your home or car before hitting the trail. A simple covering or wrap of athletic tape can prevent the friction that causes blisters; use enough tape that it won't come off during the hike but not so much that it constricts your boot's fit and not so tight that it impedes blood circulation. Sensitize yourself to recognizing when you're developing a hot spot on a foot without removing your boot and sock to confirm it; sometimes just changing your stride or pace slightly will slow a blister's development enough to get you through a hike.

If forced to remove a boot and sock to treat a blister, find a spot as protected from wind and precipitation as possible; have companions hold up jackets or pack covers to shelter your foot, if necessary. Stick your sock inside your jacket or shirt to keep it warm; if possible, do the same with your boot or its removable inner liner (if it has one). Deal with the blister as quickly and efficiently as possible, then get your sock and boot back on. If possible, treat the blister as you would in warmer weather (see later). If you feel it's safe to expose your foot to the elements only briefly, then quickly throw some tape or other protective covering over the blister to make it comfortable enough to walk. In severe windchill, don't risk taking off your boot and sock—better to walk out on a bleeding blister than to suffer frostbite.

Complete and proper blister treatment consists of the following.

Drain the blister before continuing. Clean it with an antiseptic towelette (don't mess with soap and water in winter), then dry it. Sterilize a needle or sharp blade over a flame until hot, and puncture the bottom end of the blister to drain it. Starting at the top of the blister, massage the fluid toward the hole. Apply antibiotic ointment to prevent infection, then cover it with a blister-dressing product like moleskin or something similar.

A bit of tincture of benzoin around the wound helps the dressing stick to the skin. Cut a circular piece of moleskin a half-inch bigger than the blister. Cut a hole slightly larger than the blister in the middle of the moleskin and place this "doughnut" over the blister. Cover the entire doughnut with a second piece of moleskin and/or enough tape to keep everything in place.

Hypothermia

Many hikers are familiar with this term, though not everyone fully understands what it means. **Hypothermia** occurs progressively as your body core temperature drops in response to your body losing heat to the environment faster than it can produce heat. By definition, hypothermia is a core body temperature below 95 degrees Fahrenheit (normal is around 98.6 degrees). A victim at that body temperature loses the ability to solve problems (the brain is the organ most susceptible to the effects of hypothermia, with the loss of normal thought processes setting in early); stumbles; becomes apathetic; slurs speech; has pale, cool skin; and is cold and shivering. As body core temperature continues to drop, shivering grows more violent, the victim grows more incoherent and confused, and coordination declines significantly. Eventually, the victim becomes severely hypothermic: unable to walk, no longer shivering, turns blue, and appears to have no pulse or respiration. This person cannot warm himself or herself and will die without treatment.

We know how to avoid hypothermia: proper clothing and amounts of food and fluids and movement to generate heat. The great challenges are recognizing the onset of mild hypothermia, recognizing the circumstances that elevate the risk of hypothermia, and making appropriate decisions in reaction to those circumstances.

In winter, allowing mild hypothermia to commence puts you behind the eight ball because it's difficult to treat it quickly in a winter environment, and your party is forced to redirect time, attention, and energy from the task of reaching your destination to dealing with the person with hypothermia. To head it off, train yourself to think about circumstances that can bring on hypothermia before it sets in. Any number of situations can instigate hypothermia, including the following:

- ▲ Going abruptly from a situation in which you're sweating hard (hiking uphill protected from wind) to a situation where you're exerting less and more exposed to cold wind and/or precipitation (hiking along a ridge or descending from a summit)
- ▲ The onset of wet precipitation, especially in combination with strong wind
- ▲ An abrupt drop in ambient air temperature (such as occurs around sunset)
- ▲ Inadequate consumption of food and fluids in combination with any of the earlier scenarios
- ▲ Clothing that is inadequate for any of the first three scenarios

Before entering any situation that greatly increases your chances of getting cold, assess whether everyone is prepared for it in terms of feeling warm, having a high energy level, having the proper clothing, and, importantly, having the desire to do it. Doubt, apprehension, and emotional discomfort may stem from some degree of physical discomfort—thus, possibly an early signal that someone is getting cold. Unless everyone is ready for it, do not place yourselves in a situation of increased exposure to cold wind and weather.

Recognize early clues that you are, or a companion is, getting cold: (1) a chilled feeling either while you're still moving or as soon as you stop moving; (2) a hunched posture in the shoulders or arms crossed; (3) an apparent drop in energy level and amount of movement (someone getting cold often starts walking more slowly and speaking less, or while resting either stands still or at most stamps the feet slowly in place); and (4) cold or numb fingers and toes. Address the problem immediately by first getting more clothing on the person, then providing a big drink and food, then increasing the person's exertion level (hike faster, or hike for 5 minutes up a hill to warm up). If you're in a place exposed to cold wind or weather, consider options for getting to protected terrain as quickly as possible.

If increasing food and water intake, increasing exertion level, and adding clothing don't warm up a person with hypothermia—or the victim is unable to move fast enough to begin warming up—a more drastic response becomes necessary. Depending on how far hypothermia has progressed, it may be as simple as finding a protected spot and getting the victim into a sleeping bag; it's imperative that the person be insulated from the cold ground (using a pad or packs). Someone suffering from severe hypothermia requires extreme treatment measures immediately.

The recommended treatment for a victim of severe hypothermia in the backcountry is to place the person in a hypothermia wrap: Spread out a tarp, tent rainfly, or something similarly wind- and waterproof. Lay a sleeping pad on it for insulation. Put the person in a sleeping bag on the pad. Place bottles of warm water or chemical heat packs in the person's hands and around the torso, neck, and groin (be sure to follow instructions for using chemical heat packs; some pose a threat of burn injury if used improperly). Close the person up in the bag, leaving a breathing hole. Finally, wrap the windproof layer over the top of the person, ensuring that he or she is completely enclosed within this cocoon except for the breathing hole. Don't feed or give fluids to someone incapable of swallowing. Leave one or more party members with the person while others go for help.

Emergency medical professionals have a saying: "You're not dead until you're warm and dead." A victim of severe hypothermia may be cold to the touch and have no detectable pulse or respiration but actually still be alive; it's possible that person can be revived and survive. Never presume a hypothermia victim to be dead until attempts at resuscitation and warming fail. In the backcountry, continue efforts to warm the victim until help arrives.

Unfortunately, day hikers often don't carry everything described earlier for assembling a hypothermia wrap. If the hypothermia victim is unable to continue walking out, you have to improvise as best as possible. Use all clothing available without endangering other party members and whatever materials are available to insulate the victim from the cold ground. Wrap the person in a windproof, insulated cocoon— use a tarp, emergency space blanket, bivy bag, or even an improvised snow shelter (see Chapter 10). If possible, create a cocoon that resembles a sleeping bag, enclosing the victim's entire body inside the insulation rather than isolating body parts like arms and legs as happens when we put on jackets and pants.

Frostbite

When skin tissue cools or freezes because of the loss of circulation to that part of the body, it's known as **frostbite.** The most common mechanism is the brain cutting off the flow of blood to a body part that's already cold to prevent cooled blood from reaching vital organs. Frostbite also occurs when a physical obstruction, like a compound bone fracture, impedes circulation. It usually occurs in temperatures below freezing. The warning signs include skin that feels cold, looks pale, and/or hurts. As freezing progresses, the skin gets paler and the pain ceases, then the skin grows as hard as ice and sometimes looks purple.

As with hypothermia (which frequently precedes frostbite), avoid frostbite by dressing properly—especially hand wear and footwear, because the feet and hands are most susceptible, along with the face and ears—and consuming enough food and water. Don't impede circulation by tying boots too tightly, wearing boots that are too small or clothing that's too tight, or wrapping digits too tightly in tape or a bandage. Wind combined with freezing temperatures increases the risk of frostbite. Tobacco use constricts blood vessels, increasing the risk of frostbite.

Superficial frostbite, the less serious form, is characterized by numbness, pale color, cold but pliable skin, and sharp pain when the skin thaws. It heals completely and can be treated in the backcountry by warming the cold body part through contact with warm skin—for example, by stuffing hands under your armpit, or placing cold feet against a companion's warm torso. Avoid massaging cold skin; it can damage cells. If a blister (called a *bleb*) forms after the skin is warmed, do not pop it. Keep the area warm and get medical attention. Ibuprofen reduces the risk of blood clots that can worsen frostbite.

Much more dangerous is *deep frostbite,* the symptoms of which include skin that is numb, cold, white, and frozen solid and that eventually blackens. It often results in the loss of the body part. Anyone suffering deep frostbite must be evacuated to a hospital as quickly as possible. Insulate the victim to prevent further freezing of skin. You may attempt to warm a solidly frozen body part while in the backcountry—but only if there's no danger of it refreezing again, which would be extremely painful for the victim—and only if the victim doesn't need to keep walking to reach a hospital. A frostbite victim can walk on a frozen foot but a thawed foot is too painful.

Raynaud's Disease

In 1862 Maurice Raynaud described the symptoms of a condition that would eventually bear his name and that included intense pain lasting from 5 minutes to an hour or more and a change in skin color from white to blue to rosy red. Physicians still don't know the cause but now know that the symptoms are triggered by spasms in the peripheral blood vessels of the fingers and toes and occasionally the ears and nose. Persons with Raynaud's disease experience pain with a slight drop in temperature. Various treatments—avoidance of cold, tranquilizers, vasodilating drugs, hormones, biofeedback—have met limited success. If you think you have

Raynaud's disease, talk to your physician. In about 10 percent of cases, the symptoms are indicative of an underlying disease.

I have this problem and deal with it through these techniques:

▲ Staying hydrated and snacking frequently

▲ Keeping my entire body warm, so that the body moves blood to the extremities

▲ Layering gloves and mittens for warmth and versatility and wearing warm, waterproof boots and warm socks

▲ Never exposing bare hands to cold air more than briefly and sticking hands in my pants to warm them when necessary

Immersion Foot

Known to soldiers of past generations as *trench foot,* this condition is brought on by the feet remaining wet and cold for a prolonged period, several hours or more, which causes vasoconstriction of the skin capillaries, shutting off blood flow. What is a normal physiological defense mechanism to prevent excessive loss of body heat can result in damage to the skin if it persists for about 12 hours of more. Temperatures don't have to be below freezing for immersion foot to develop, but the foot does have to be cold as well as wet.

Proper footwear that keeps your feet warm and dry is the obvious prevention for immersion foot, that is, waterproof boots and thick wool or synthetic socks in winter, with gaiters or pants that keep snow and water out of your boots. Even if your boots and/or socks get wet, well-insulated boots and warm socks can continue to keep your feet warm enough to avoid this condition.

Immersion foot becomes painful once the foot begins to warm up again. Treat it in the backcountry by gently drying the foot, warming it, and putting on dry footwear, if possible. Elevate the foot and massage it gently to reduce swelling, which can be severe. Aspirin or ibuprofen can help alleviate the pain. If the victim is capable of walking out, he or she may do so. The victim should see a physician as soon as possible.

Falls and Trauma Injuries

This broad category includes an array of injuries, among them bone fractures; soft-tissue injuries (cuts, abrasions, puncture wounds); sprains; strains; and head, neck, and spinal injuries. I lump them together to emphasize caution in the winter environment to avoid the mechanism of injury for all of these—usually, a slip or stumble. At any time of year, these injuries are most common later in the day, when we're tired and often less attentive; in winter, the risk of such injuries goes up any time of day that we're traveling over slippery surfaces. Recognizing that a fall can happen anytime and concentrating on moving safely, especially when walking on a slippery surface like snow, ice, mud, or wet rocks, is the best way to avoid such accidents.

Falls are more likely when walking downhill because, whereas when walking uphill our body weight is centered over the foot onto which we're stepping, when walking downhill we're often landing on a foot that's out in front of our body weight, or our center of balance. In addition, we're often moving faster going downhill. Try to focus on taking short steps and keeping your weight above your landing foot. On dry or wet ground, or firm snow or ice, walk in a slightly zigzagging pattern (as if creating your own switchbacks within the trail), so that your feet are diagonal to the fall line, which places more foot surface in contact with the ground for improved purchase. In softer snow, land heavily onto your heels with each downhill step to bury your heels deeply enough into the snow to prevent them from slipping out ahead of you. Keeping your weight back slightly (though not too far back), rather than forward, helps ensure that you land on your butt and pack if you slip, which is virtually always safer than pitching forward downhill. Using ski or adjustable trekking poles, or an ice ax if the terrain calls for it, greatly aids balance. Don't move so fast that you stumble and trip.

Ultimately, falls are not completely avoidable, so we must be prepared to deal with an injury in freezing temperatures. When a fall results in significant pain, or someone falls from a height of more than a few feet or lands on the head, stop and assess whether the person has suffered an injury.

Of foremost concern are injuries to the head and spinal cord, which should be presumed following a serious fall or loss of consciousness until you can confirm otherwise. Never move a patient with a potential spinal-cord injury before the neck and spine are stabilized, unless the victim and/or rescuers are faced with an immediate environmental threat to life, like falling rock or avalanche. Stabilize the victim's neck and spine to prevent movement by having one party member kneel by the victim's head and gently cradle the head and neck. Immobilize the victim's neck and spine using whatever materials are available: clothing, a piece of foam pad folded in half lengthwise for rigidity, or other improvised materials wrapped around the patient's neck and secured in place with tape or knotted strips of fabric. Anyone with a potential head or spinal cord injury should be evacuated to a hospital as soon as possible. A head-injury victim might be able to walk out under his or her own power, but a potential spinal-injury victim must be carried out.

Check for signs of bleeding, which is easy to initially overlook if it's hidden beneath layers of clothing and the victim is still feeling an adrenalin rush after the fall; also, someone who is cold may not notice any bleeding. Look for dark stains appearing in clothing and feel for unusual dampness. Don't open or remove clothing unless there's a suspicion of bleeding—you don't want to make the victim cold; but if there's any reason to suspect bleeding, such as torn clothing, conduct a thorough inspection for a bleeding wound, even if it means removing clothing. Stop the bleeding by applying direct, flat pressure to the wound; it may take some time, but pressure will virtually always stop bleeding. The only situation where applying pressure is not appropriate is when it could danger-ously impede circulation, such as in the neck; try pinching off that type of wound instead. Clean an open wound by flushing it with sterile water (tap water or bottled water should be fine) as long as you don't risk freezing the victim's skin, then bandage it.

Sharp localized pain may indicate a bad bruise or a bone fracture. In a joint, it may also indicate a sprain, which is the overstretching or tearing of ligaments that support the bones around a joint like the ankle. In a muscle, pain may indicate a strain or muscle tear. All of these injuries can be debilitating, although in some cases the victim may still be able to walk after an injury of these types to a leg. It can be hard to distinguish a bad sprain from a fracture unless you're trained to evaluate such injuries or the victim actually hears and/or feels a bone break. Muscles spasms around the injury or the feeling of broken bone scraping together (called *crepitus*) are symptoms of a fracture. Either type of injury can cause significant pain and swelling.

Treat a bruise or swelling immediately with RICE, an acronym that means *R*est, *I*ce (a chemical ice pack, snow, immersing the swollen area in cold water, or wrapping the injured body part in a wet shirt), *C*ompression (wrapping the injured part, not too tightly, in an elastic bandage or an unused shirt), and *E*levation above the heart to reduce swelling. Periodically check to make sure a bandage or compres-sion wrap of an injury doesn't cut off circulation beyond the bandage. A bone fracture may require a splint to stabilize the broken bone by immobilizing the joints above and below the break, or if the break is in a joint, immobilizing that joint. Apply ice to a muscle strain. If you're not carrying a first-aid kit with a splint, improvise with whatever is available, such as a ski pole or sturdy stick. An antiin-flammatory like ibuprofen helps reduce pain and inflammation. After some rest—its length depending on the severity of the injury and your circumstances—the victim may be able to, or have to, walk out on his or her own.

Sunburn and Snow Blindness

Despite winter's shorter days and lower sun angle, the threat of sunburn can be greater than in summer. A sunny day combined with snow-covered ground (which reflects most sunlight) and a prolonged period spent above tree line, especially at high altitude where there's less atmosphere to shield your skin from ultraviolet (UV) rays, can be harmful to your skin. Don't take UV exposure lightly. In 1930 an American's chance of developing melanoma was 1 in 1500; today, it is 1 in 75, partly because of the increased popularity of outdoor recreation. According to one estimate, someone dies of melanoma every hour in this country. **Snow blindness**—which is sunburn to the cornea—is debilitating and painful, even if only a temporary condition.

In cold temperatures, we're wearing tightly woven clothing for warmth, any-way, which is the best protection against UV rays. Frequently apply sunblock

Always protect your eyes during winter excursions. In extreme cold, goggles are necessary to protect the eyes from literally freezing shut. On sunny days, wear full-coverage sunglasses that protect your eyes from ultraviolet rays when on snow-covered ground.

with a high skin protection factor (SPF) rating to all uncovered skin, including in and behind your ears and inside your nostrils, all areas that can burn from UV rays reflected off snow. When possible, wear a hat that shades your head and neck, and always wear full-coverage sunglasses to protect your eyes from the internal burning that can cause temporary snow blindness and to reduce the chance of cataracts later in life. Protect children from excessive sun exposure— 80 percent of skin damage from the sun happens before age 20, although it usually doesn't appear for 30 years. You can take infants out in winter (see Chapter 4), but shield them from the sun.

Sunburn is characterized by red, dry, peeling, possibly blistered skin that's sensitive. Treat sunburn by avoiding more sun, drinking a lot of water, and applying moisturizing lotion for comfort. Apply cool, wet compresses to snow-blind eyes, and perhaps a small amount of antibiotic ointment under the eyelid, and cover up the eyes, if possible, for 24 hours.

Altitude Illness

Symptoms of **altitude illness,** or **acute mountain sickness (AMS),** can appear at 8000 feet or lower in people not acclimatized. There are different types of AMS, and symptoms can resemble severe dehydration, hypothermia, or flu. They include a painful headache, difficulty breathing, loss of appetite, nausea, and unnatural weariness. An advanced symptom is ataxia, or a drunklike loss of coordination. AMS can be fatal, particularly two conditions of advanced altitude sickness known as *high altitude pulmonary edema (HAPE)* and *high altitude cerebral edema (HACE)*. HAPE reveals itself in extremely labored breathing and the sound of gurgling, and HACE with severe headache, a rapidly deteriorating level of consciousness, and sometimes hallucinations.

Avoid AMS by spending the necessary time acclimatizing (that is, slowly advancing to higher altitudes to allow the body to adjust to the reduced amount of oxygen drawn in each breath). The "necessary time" depends on your own biological capacity for acclimating, which you cannot predict but can learn through experience. Your fitness level does not affect your ability to acclimatize, and you may find that an altitude that does not bother you on one trip makes you ill on a subsequent trip (perhaps owing to other health factors). Above roughly 8000 or 10,000 feet, sleep no more than 1000 feet higher each night, and hike to an altitude each day than you will sleep that night. Remember that cold, dry air dehydrates you quickly, and your body's fluid needs rise with the elevation, so drink plenty of water. Ultimately, though, everyone has a limit on how high they can go before experiencing AMS symptoms.

Treatment is simple: Rest at your current altitude if symptoms wane, but if not, descend. The drug acetazolamide, sold by prescription under the name Diamox, can reduce symptoms of altitude illness and facilitate acclimatization. Persons showing symptoms of HAPE or HACE should be brought down immediately and taken to a hospital.

Managing Emergencies

The winter environment can introduce many complications to hinder the management of an emergency. As at any other time of year, certain guidelines should dictate your decisions:

    1. Let one person take charge, to ensure the efficient coordination of everyone's

efforts. Decide right away who that should be, preferably based on wilderness first-aid experience.

2. Take a head count. Make sure no one is missing. Another injured person may be hidden from view.

3. Never create more injured people. Survey the scene for immediate environmental threats, such as falling rock, avalanche, or thin ice. Don't move a victim who may have a spinal-cord injury unless the environment poses an immediate threat.

4. Conduct a primary patient assessment: Confirm that the victim has an open airway, is breathing, and has a pulse. The lack of any of these is immediately life threatening and must be addressed right away by clearing the airway and performing rescue breathing and/or cardiopulmonary resuscitation (CPR). Many communities offer inexpensive CPR courses.

5. Following the primary survey, conduct a secondary survey to determine the victim's injuries. He or she may be able to tell you exactly what's wrong, but don't assume so, because cold and adrenalin can mask pain. If necessary, carefully examine the victim with your hands from head to toe, palpating body parts to check for pain, bleeding, and broken bones. Check for sensation in the feet and fingers; lack of sensation suggests the possibility of nerve damage, spinal-cord injury, or circulation impeded by a broken bone or swelling. Note whether skin is dry, moist, or clammy and its color and temperature. Check for normal capillary refill by squeezing the victim's fingertips and toes (the latter only if it's deemed safe to remove boots) between your thumb and forefinger for several seconds; if the digit does not return to a healthy pink color within two seconds after releasing it, circulation is impaired.

6. Take detailed notes on the victim's condition, including monitoring and recording pulse and respiratory rate and the victim's level of consciousness every 5 minutes—especially if the level of consciousness changes for the worse. Record what is known as a *SAMPLE history: s*ymptoms, *a*llergies, *m*edications the victim is taking, *p*ast medical history, *l*ast food and fluids consumed, and *e*vents leading up to the accident. These notes will be delivered to medical professionals.

7. During the secondary survey, make the victim warm and comfortable and insulate him or her from the ground with a pad or pack to the extent possible without risking neck or spinal injury. Stabilize the injuries using methods advised earlier and prepare a plan for evacuating the injured, whether under the victim's own power or being carried.

8. If immediate evacuation is not feasible because of your party size or other factors, improvise a shelter from whatever materials are available while other party members go for help. (See the "Getting Benighted" section in Chapter 4 and Chapter 10 for information about snow shelters.)

Remember this: The earlier guidelines are just that, guidelines. Subjective judgments are made in real-world situations. The winter environment may make it impossible to follow some guidelines assiduously, such as removing any of the victim's clothing to check for bleeding or injuries. On the other hand, you may be forced to deal immediately with a severe injury, despite the environment. All you can do is exercise your best judgment, bearing in mind that any backcountry rescue is likely to take hours, if not days, therefore you need a long-term strategy for patient care.

PART II
Winter Camping

How well you plan a winter camping trip greatly affects your comfort and safety while on the trip.

Chapter 7

Trip Planning

P icture an astronaut walking in space, tethered to the spacecraft by a cable— a lifeline. The farther out the astronaut ventures from the ship, the longer that lifeline stretches out, the greater our space walker's distance from safety. I imagine that astronaut being keenly aware of his or her physical distance from the spacecraft door.

The space-walking astronaut is an apt metaphor for our adventures into the backcountry. The greater our distance from civilization—both in terms of distance and the time it takes to travel that distance—the greater, by some measures, our risk. This oversimplifies the relative risks of the outdoors, of course; but it's fair to say that heading out there in winter extends the lifeline a bit farther than going to the same place in summer. And camping out there in winter stretches the lifeline even farther.

Beginning with this chapter, I'll get into the skills and equipment needed for winter camping—above and beyond the information presented in Chapters 1 through 6, all of which still applies to the winter camper.

Choosing a Destination

Hopefully, you are bringing to your first winter camping adventures a solid body of experience as a winter day hiker, including some refinement of your skills for staying warm and dry and navigating through a wintry environment. You've developed some confidence in your ability to get around and not only survive but stay reasonably comfortable. You want to elevate the adventure a notch. So my first bit of advice may seem to contradict your objectives: Set a modest goal on those first winter camping trips.

Maybe you could go farther and push harder. However, the mere fact of spending a night outside in winter already takes you farther out than, perhaps, you've ever gone before. You don't need an ambitious agenda in terms of the distance you'll travel or number of days and nights you'll spend outside on those initial trips—the adventure and challenges await even a few miles from the road. Even for the seasoned winter hiker, camping in winter is a new activity. Surprises can happen. Better to work out the bugs in your winter camping system and skills before testing yourself. When you do start to venture farther out on the lifeline, you'll be better prepared to enjoy it.

Some general advice for the new winter camper:

▲ Introduce yourself to winter travel and camping through short overnight trips.
▲ Avoid forecasts of extremely cold or stormy weather; moderate winter conditions will be challenging enough.
▲ Plan an itinerary that includes escape routes for a quick retreat in case things go wrong and be prepared to alter your itinerary if the situation demands it.
▲ Choose a destination you've been to previously, either on a winter day hike or a backpacking trip during warmer months.
▲ Remember that traveling little-used trails or off-trail can present greater navigational challenges than hiking popular trails. As you get into truly remote wilderness, where you're unlikely to encounter any other parties in winter, you place yourself in a situation of absolute self-sufficiency, which demands expert skills.
▲ Think hard about the month you choose for your winter-camping trip. Early winter, December and January, have shorter days and are usually much colder than late February and March. In a place with a harsh winter climate, consider making your first multi-day "winter" trip in April or November, which can provide great training for true winter conditions.
▲ Find out whether overnight camping is permitted at your chosen destination and whether there are restrictions on camping in winter that may not apply in other seasons.

As you gain experience and yearn for greater challenges, ramp up the difficulty level of your trips gradually. Longer trips—both in distance traveled and the number of days and nights—extend your lifeline farther and farther. Just as you think about your distance from civilization (and advanced medical care) during a day hike, think about it on a multi-day trip, realizing that often the time it would take for you to get back out to civilization in the event of an emergency multiplies exponentially compared with day hikes.

Multi-day trips can bring us into terrain infrequently visited by other people—because it lies beyond the reach of day hikers—meaning we're often breaking our

A campsite in the woods, such as this site on the Appalachian Trail in Maine, offers much more protection from wind than camping in the open.

own trail, which slows us down dramatically. We cannot assume the kindness of strangers will be available if we need help.

Multi-day trips take a cumulative physical toll. We're more tired after a few days or more of laboring in the winter backcountry than at the trip's outset, affecting everything from our energy level, stamina, and speed of travel to the energy reserves our bodies have for keeping us warm and our ability to deal with unexpected problems.

Longer trips can take a cumulative mental toll, as well. It's hard being in the freezing and possibly wet, snowy wilderness day after day. Carrying a heavy pack for multiple days in cold temperatures places greater physical demands on your body than a day hike. Make sure your entire party is in shape for it, physically and mentally.

Keep an open mind to the itinerary before and during the trip, and adjust it if needed. You don't have to pack up and move every day: Given the shorter days of winter and greater time needed to do just about everything, sometimes it's more fun to set up a base camp for more than one night and take day trips exploring from there.

Choosing Partners

To the novice, deciding whom to invite on a backcountry trip may seem obvious: whatever friends are available. As we take more trips of a committing and demanding nature, we develop a finer appreciation of the importance of selecting the right companions—that choosing your partners may be the most important decision you make before or during the trip.

Not everyone shares the same ambition, stamina, emotional comfort level, or personal definition of what level of risk or discomfort are acceptable. (This book presumes as much in its format, addressing winter hikers separately from winter campers.) Some people learn this lesson the hard way, inviting the wrong people on a trip that turns into a disaster because not everyone is up to the trip's challenges. When someone can't keep up, it's not fun for that person or the party's stronger, more-experienced members who get slowed down by the slower member, and it's potentially dangerous for everyone.

To avoid unpleasant trips, for starters, involve everyone in the planning. There is a tendency for less-experienced people to leave all decisions about the trip itinerary to the more-experienced party members, which can result in unwanted surprises in the backcountry. When everyone gets involved in the planning, everyone gets a clear idea of what's in store, and individuals can—and should—speak up when they see something they don't think they can handle.

Similarly, involve everyone in decision-making while in the backcountry. Don't presume to know what's best for everyone or that someone else knows the limits of your abilities or desire. Don't follow someone into a situation that makes you uncomfortable to the point of feeling unsafe or coax someone into doing something they don't believe they can do.

As your adventures grow more serious and demanding, your pool of partners will grow smaller—but that's good. You should be more selective about your partners on committing trips. You'll be safest and most successful, and you'll have the most fun when accompanied by people who understand and are prepared for whatever you encounter.

Chapter 8

Clothing and Gear for Camping

t never fails to amaze me how much heavier my pack gets for a multi-day winter trip compared with a summer backpacking trip of the same duration. Not only do you need more food in winter but clothing and gear needs naturally increase when you're going to spend a night or more outside in temperatures well below freezing. This chapter covers the additional clothing and gear needed for winter camping (see Chapter 2 for basic clothing and gear needed for winter hiking).

The Clothing

Plan your winter camping ensemble with the same efficiency as you do your clothing for any other outing. Beyond what's recommended in Chapter 2, you need clothing that insulates well when you're sitting around not generating heat through exertion. Customize your wardrobe to meet your personal needs and the demands of the climate where you do most of your winter hiking and camping.

Select individual garments based on two criteria: (1) how well they function alone in the conditions you'll face and (2) how well they layer together with other garments you take. Although not everything fits into a layering system, ideally, most of your outdoor clothing is useful alone and in multiple combinations with other garments. With the exception of puffy insulating garments for the campsite, single-purpose articles of clothing are not efficient choices. If you find yourself on the coldest night of any trip wearing virtually every stitch of clothing you brought, and you're warm, then you have chosen your wardrobe well.

Avoid excessive redundancy between garments—for example, you don't need two jackets that are waterproof-breathable (W-B); but one W-B shell and one lightweight wind shell or soft shell cover a wide range of weather conditions and, if chosen correctly, can be layered together.

Choose your clothing according to the circumstances of your trip. On short trips you may pack more frugally, taking just one jersey and one or two pairs of socks, for instance; whereas on longer outings of many days, you may want spare items (especially hand wear and socks). The amount of warm, insulating clothing you bring will be dictated by the coldest temperatures you could encounter and how easily you get cold. Never shortchange yourself on warm

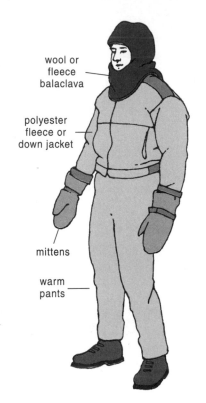

wool or fleece balaclava

polyester fleece or down jacket

mittens

warm pants

Illustration 8-1: Warm insulating layers from head to feet keep you warm by trapping body heat. (From Cox, Steven M., and Kris Fulsaas, eds. *Mountaineering: The Freedom of the Hills.* 7th ed. Seattle: The Mountaineers Books, 2003.)

clothing; it is worth the few extra pounds and added bulk. In addition, extra warm clothing can be used to supplement a sleeping bag that would otherwise be not warm enough for winter camping—elite climbers and some weekend winter warriors choose to shave ounces by carrying a three-season bag and just wearing more clothing to bed. If there's a possibility of temperatures swinging above and below freezing, which can put your clothing through cycles of getting wet and freezing, it may be impossible to keep the clothing you wear on the trail dry, so think about keeping a spare set of base layers dry in your pack for the campsite.

Consider these general tips on categories of clothing for winter camping:

▲ Modern base layers can be worn for multiple days on end without losing their shape or functionality or even getting terribly smelly, in part because they move moisture and dry out so quickly. The only reasons for carrying more than one base layer—that is, a shirt, underwear, and long underwear—are if you need base layers of different weights for varying temperatures or if, on a wet trip, you want to keep a spare change of base layers dry in your pack for wearing in camp.

▲ With insulating clothing, thicker means warmer (Illustration 8-1). Much of today's technical clothing is closer fitting than past generations, without compromising much warmth. These garments are more efficient at trapping heat with less bulk, so a less bulky modern fleece jacket may be comparable to a much bulkier fleece jacket from 10 years ago. Still, close-fitting garments have less air volume inside, and it's the pockets of air in clothing, warmed by our body heat, that provide insulation against the cold. In short, thicker still means warmer, and nothing beats a fat down or synthetic jacket for warmth, period.

My own comfort when winter camping improved greatly when I broke down and bought a good down jacket. The best of them are fat and yet compact in a stuff sack, thanks to continued improvements in the quality of down and synthetic fills, and have deep, insulated pockets for warming hands quickly, a shell that's water-resistant, and sometimes a hood (although a hood may be unnecessarily redundant with your other head layers). In pants, the choice is generally between heavyweight fleece and synthetic-fill pants, the latter being less bulky when packed. Synthetic fills are better for long trips, when moisture from your body can build up inside a jacket, because synthetic fills, as you know, are warmer when wet than down.

▲ Warm camp booties were the other item, besides a down jacket, that greatly improved my comfort when camping in winter. Booties come with either down or synthetic fill, and there's little difference in packability because they're a relatively small item, anyway. The alternative for warm camp footwear is an extra pair of insulating liners for your double boots (assuming you're using boots with a removable liner); you can pull stuff sacks or plastic bags over the liners for walking on snow. The advantage of liners is they pull double duty if your primary pair of liners gets wet, but they are bulkier and heavier than booties. And booties are a little more comfortable to wear inside a sleeping bag than boot liners.

▲ Carrying a variety of head wear not only allows you choices to avoid overheating or getting cold while on the trail but head layers provide a lot of insulation for a relatively small amount of fabric. On many winter camping trips, I'll carry a windproof earband, a lightweight hat or base layer balaclava (either of which is more versatile if you can roll it up to cover or uncover your ears as desired), and a warmer hat or expedition-weight balaclava. And, of course, your shell jacket should have a full-coverage hood with an ample brim to keep weather off your head, face, and neck.

▲ The longer your trip, the more important it is to carry spare gloves or mittens and extra socks. Even on short trips, I carry a variety of gloves and mittens, which

When going downhill, your exertion level and body heat production both drop; add layers, including a warm hat, to stay warm.

preferably can be layered together in various combinations, because my fingers get cold easily and I like having dry hand wear available to change into when needed. Good socks can be worn for more than one day, especially in cold, dry weather. In wet weather—and temperatures around and/or above freezing— frequently change socks to avoid immersion foot or frostbite (see Chapter 6).

▲ On a multi-day trip, bring an extra pair of sunglasses. They add negligible weight and bulk to your load, and it's easy to break or lose your primary pair of shades. You are less likely to break or lose goggles, but you may want a back-up pair on an extended trip in deep cold.

The Gear

Pack

For starters, you'll need a bigger pack for multi-day winter trips because you'll need a greater amount of clothing, food, and gear in winter. The capacity required depends on the length of your trip, how cold it may get, and how bulky your clothing and gear is—for example, whether your sleeping bag is a compact, five-degree Fahrenheit down bag with fill rated at 800 or 900, or an older, bulkier below–twenty-degree bag with synthetic fill, and whether you carry a roomy tent or a bivy bag.

The best way to determine the capacity needed is to throw all the clothing and gear you'll take winter camping into a duffel, bring it to your outdoor gear retailer, and load it into any pack you're considering buying. You may be surprised by how much space it occupies. If you'll carry a winter bag, clothing for camping in temperatures around zero degrees Fahrenheit, and your share of a winter tent, you may fill a pack in the 4000 to 5000 cubic inch range for trips ranging from a weekend to a week. Get enough capacity for your trips—attaching things to the outside of a pack can make the load unwieldy and subject those items to weather and environmental damage from things like sharp branches. But don't get more pack than you need—you'll just be tempted to fill it up, which can put you in the bad habit of bringing more stuff than you need.

The importance of comfort and load control does not diminish in winter—arguably those characteristics of a pack become more critical. Yes, the warm clothing you wear provides some padding, reducing somewhat the need for thick padding in a pack's hipbelt and shoulder straps. However, there may be times you're hiking in shirtsleeves in winter, so don't skimp too much on padding. Traveling on snow can be challenging; you don't want your pack shifting or not fitting well. The bigger and heavier a pack, the more important that it fit well. Packs with adjustable harnesses can often be fitted precisely to your torso, whereas packs that are not adjustable (fixed suspension systems, or harnesses) typically fit a narrow range of torso lengths. Fixed suspensions are usually lighter than adjustable ones, though, so if you can find one that fits well, it may be a good choice. Some packs come with more than one size of hipbelt and harness/shoulder straps to help customize the fit, and there are women's models designed to fit female hips and torso dimensions. Look for external and internal compression straps that prevent the pack's contents from shifting even when the pack is partially filled. The pack should hug your back without shifting side to side even when you slip on snow, which makes an internal-frame pack more practical in winter than an external frame.

Pack heavy items low and toward the rear of a sled so it doesn't flip or nose into the snow.

Good organization and compartmentalization is valuable in a multi-day back-pack for winter—you don't want to stand around in the cold looking for something. But too many external pockets and doodads can get in the way of attaching snowshoes or skis (compression straps and/or specialized external features should hold those securely) and make a pack too wide and bulky, moving weight away from your back to the outside of the pack. Find a streamlined pack with only the features you want, nothing superfluous, and get in the habit of organizing items in stuff sacks within the pack.

Pay attention to and compare the weight of packs when empty, and don't carry more weight than necessary. Remember that whereas some packs are lighter because of lightweight materials, often you're compromising some support and comfort in the suspension system and certain features. A lightweight pack is smart for moderate loads. If you get a lightweight pack and then proceed to put fifty pounds or more into it, you may find it uncomfortable. Your pack's suspension should be designed for the weight you plan to put in the pack.

Sled

Talk to anyone who's pulled a gear sled, and you'll hear the same thing: A sled can be your best friend and your worst enemy. Pulling a sled full of gear instead of lugging a heavy pack transfers much of the load from your back to the snow-covered ground, allowing you to take more gear with less effort—provided you choose the situations in which you use a sled wisely.

On a multi-day trip, a sled gets some of the load off your back. Sleds should only be used on flat or gently rolling terrain—not on steep ground.

Sleds work best on flat or gently rolling terrain. If you're heading for the hills, carry a pack instead.

A sled can hold a lot. Resist the temptation to bring the kitchen sink, because you still have to haul that thing. Pack the heaviest items low and toward the rear of the sled to make it less likely to flip or nose into the snow.

Make sure there's reliable snow coverage on the ground; if it's thin, or melting opens up bare ground during your trip (which may happen at lower elevations), you could be struggling to drag a sled over rocks, dirt, or mud.

If you're breaking trail through deep powder, a sled whose base is wider than the track created by your skis or snowshoes will tend to ride up onto one side of the track and frequently tip over. Narrow, streamlined sleds work better in backcountry snow. When breaking trail on skis, maintain a slightly wide stride, because snow tends to collapse into a fresh track, narrowing it. When breaking trail on snowshoes, have the second person step beside, rather than in, the prints left by the lead person to create a flatter track that's easier for sled hauling.

If you're pulling the sled with a hipbelt or harness, make sure it's well padded. If you're carrying a pack while pulling a sled, buckling a sled hipbelt over a pack hipbelt can be uncomfortable and insecure. Instead, use carabiners to clip the poles to the pack's hipbelt near your hipbones (rather than clipping to the back of your pack), to minimize forward-backward sled tug against your body.

Solid poles that flex slightly, crossed between you and the front of the sled in an X-shape, keep it from slamming into your heels going downhill and help it stay in your ski or snowshoe track, whereas stiff poles can pull the sled out of the track in corners. If your sled doesn't have a harness and poles, 4 to 6 feet of PVC pipe with 5 mm or 6 mm accessory cord strung through them work well.

If deep, unconsolidated snow makes breaking trail with a sled in tow impossible, consider alternative strategies: (1) Lighten the load of the person breaking trail by shifting gear from his or her sled to others or (2) take short shifts breaking trail without a sled—the leader leaving the sled behind while breaking trail, then doubling back to retrieve it while a second party member repeats the procedure. Either method will slow you down but may be the only option in difficult conditions.

Tent

Winter often presents us with a choice among three general types of shelter: a tent, a bivy bag, and a snow shelter. The advantages of a tent over a snow shelter are that it's portable and much faster and easier to put up; and although it's obviously heavier and bulkier than a bivy bag, a tent provides vastly more comfortable accommodations. For most winter camping trips, a tent is the preferred alternative.

A winter tent must have the strength and stability to stand up under the weight of snow and the abuse of strong winds, especially when camping in open terrain. ▶

A winter tent should keep out the elements and shrug off strong winds and heavy snow. It should also ventilate well to release the moisture we exhale during the night, which can collect on the tent ceiling and walls, freezing and making the tent heavier to carry, and possibly melting and dripping onto its occupants. Winter tents are usually heavier than three-season tents because of the greater number of poles, having more solid fabric than mesh, and often because they are bigger to provide more interior space. They are often more expensive than three-season tents.

Sometimes models that manufacturers call *mountaineering tents* have many of the characteristics ideal for winter, but look closely, because in the interest of shaving weight, mountaineering tents are sometimes cramped inside and have a single-wall rather than a traditional double-wall design. Here are some things to look for in a winter tent:

- A minimum of three poles and as many as five, made of aluminum, high-strength aluminum, or carbon fiber (fiberglass shatters easily). More poles mean greater stability.
- Good ventilation, including zippered or retractable vents that can be opened in any weather without letting precipitation inside; two doors for cross-ventilation; and two-way zippers on the doors, with a hood over the door and/or a drip line that keeps precipitation out of the tent when you open the rainfly door, so you can crack doors open.
- Multiple points for staking and guying out the tent.
- Enough interior space for extra clothing and some gear and to keep bags and you from brushing against the walls if condensation builds up. In winter, I often take a tent built for one more person than my party's size—for example, a three-person tent for two people—for the extra space.
- An aerodynamic profile. Tall, vertical tent walls catch strong winds, stressing poles and fabric. Larger tents with big walls often can't help but catch wind, but with solid stitching and construction, sturdy poles, and plenty of guy-out points, it should survive strong gusts.
- A rainfly extending nearly to the ground and that optionally attaches to the poles (usually via clips or hook-and-loop closures).
- Enough vestibule space (preferably in two vestibules) for cooking and storing gear and wet clothing.
- Two doors are preferable to one for many reasons: (1) in case the wind direction changes during a snowstorm and you want to get out without letting blowing snow in, (2) easier entry and exit without climbing over companions, and (3) better ventilation.
- Depending on the snow quality and likely weather, you might pack a lightweight, minimalist tent set-up that provides adequate shelter while trimming your pack weight. Some winter tent models can be pitched rainfly-only, allowing you to leave the inner tent canopy at home, shaving a few pounds. Purchasing a separate floor (or "footprint") that matches the rainfly dimensions

gives you a lightweight but effective barrier between yourself and the snow surface. Some tent models are essentially a teepee, pitching with a single center pole (often using two connected ski or trekking poles) and staking out around their perimeter. When properly pitched and guyed, shelters like these are just as strong in winds as a full winter tent but may allow snow to blow up from underneath the rainfly edges and may not trap heat inside as effectively as a standard double-wall tent. Building snow walls around the edges can help prevent or reduce snow blowing inside. A single layer of nylon between the inside air and the slightly colder outside air may also contribute to condensation buildup inside if you have to close the shelter up completely because of stormy weather. On the other hand, such a shelter will ventilate well with the door(s) open on a calm night.

▲ Some tents cross over from three-season to winter use—thus the name *convertible tents*. They have features like zip-out solid panels over large mesh windows, optional poles, and even a rainfly that rolls back, so that you can ventilate on warm nights and carry less weight on three-season trips, yet have the added structural stability and weather protection in winter. Like many items of gear that try to perform two distinctly different functions, convertible tents handle three-season and winter conditions fairly well but are not ideal for the extremes of any season. They are too warm on hot nights (unless it's dry and you can leave the rainfly off), and they are often not strong enough for the severe winds and heavy snowfall. Some also are mediocre at ventilating in warm or cold temperatures. Still, most convertible tents can handle all but the most extreme winter trips, and they're more economical than buying two tents.

▲ Lastly, because regular tent stakes pop right out of snow, you'll need snow stakes, which are usually purchased separately, although they're inexpensive. Snow stakes are wide and longer than standard three-season stakes and often shaped and perforated with holes to hold better in snow. (See Chapter 10 for more information.)

Sleeping Bag

A bag isn't just standard camping gear in temperatures well below freezing— it's emergency gear. Winter bags are generally rated zero to five degrees Fahrenheit and lower, and there's a wide range of ratings for winter bags. Choose a bag appropriate for your destination's climate. To find the right winter bag, it's important to understand bags in general.

A bag keeps you warm by trapping your body heat in tiny air pockets in the bag's fill, or insulating material. As you know already, your body is the furnace, and without enough food and water, your internal pilot light goes out and any bag might feel cold.

All sleeping bag temperature ratings are set by the bags' manufacturer, because the outdoor industry lacks a standard for measuring a bag's warmth. That's no surprise, given the variables that affect how warm you are in a bag, including how well fed and hydrated you are and your own metabolism. Bags bearing the same temperature rating can differ significantly in warmth. Despite its somewhat arbitrary nature, though, temperature rating provides a good starting point in looking for a bag. Knowing whether you get cold easily or not will help you narrow your choices. People that get cold easily may prefer a bag that's rated ten or twenty degrees lower than the coldest nighttime temperatures they expect to encounter.

Some manufacturers offer women's bags with extra insulation, because many women get cold more easily than men, and dimensions suited to female contours so that a woman isn't wasting precious body heat warming up excess bag space.

Bags are filled with one of two types of insulation: synthetic or goose down. Bags with synthetic fills are less expensive, easier to launder, and dry more quickly than comparably rated down bags, but they are heavier, bulkier, and less durable. Most significantly for winter users, synthetic fills retain much of their ability to trap heat when wet—and on wet trips or long trips in extreme cold, a lot of moisture can build up in a bag's insulation night after night simply from what you exhale and release from your pores. Polarguard 3D is the most common synthetic fill in backcountry bags because it's lighter and more compressible than others.

Down bags are lighter and more compact when stuffed than synthetic bags—and as you get into bigger bags for colder temperatures, the advantage in weight and bulk grows more distinct. Moreover, given proper care, they last longer. Yet they are more expensive than synthetic and lose their ability to keep you warm as they get wet. Down fill is rated with a number that represents the volume of space, in cubic inches, an ounce of that quality of down fills. An ounce of 800-fill down will puff up to occupy 800 cubic inches of space. The higher the fill rating, the lighter and more compact the bag for its temperature rating. Higher fill ratings also cost more.

Consider your own needs when deciding between down and synthetic. Wet trips, or long, cold trips, usually demand synthetic bags. If you're careful about keeping your bag dry, a down bag will rarely fail to keep you warm on a trip in any weather of up to a week or more. Some shell fabrics used on bags today also are highly water resistant and breathable, so they allow less environmental moisture to enter the bag and move much of your body moisture out of the bag, making those fabrics ideal for down bags.

Before buying a winter bag, take these steps:

▲ The best cursory measure of a bag's warmth is its loft, or thickness. In the store, lay out the bags on your short list and compare their fatness once they've had time to loft.

▲ Crawl inside the bag in the store and close it up. See whether it has enough space for your head, shoulders, chest, waist, and feet. Consider how much clothing you might wear inside the bag and whether it has the space for that—you may want enough space for two or three extra clothing layers, and on nights that you don't need those clothes, you likely won't mind the extra elbowroom. Don't get a bag that's roomier than you need, because you'll burn more energy heating up that excess air in the bag and can wind up feeling cold.

▲ Make sure the zipper, hood, and drawstrings are all easy to reach and manipulate.

▲ Look for a fat draft tube inside the zipper to keep out cold air, and a similar neck collar.

▲ Check out a bag's construction: Does the stitching look solid? Are there any loose threads? Does the bag's shell appear to be shedding feathers?

Most bags come in two or three lengths; find the best fit for you. In winter, you may prefer a bag that's longer than you'd use in summer, allowing you to store clothing or damp boots in the foot of the bag (to keep the clothes warm and the boots from freezing; see more in Chapter 10).

Sleeping bags don't require much maintenance, but to ensure a long life, follow these guidelines:

▲ In the backcountry, keep your bag out of the dirt and watch out for sharp objects. When possible, lay the bag out in the sun to air dry it during a trip.

▲ Wear at least a base layer of clothing, top and bottom, and a hat when sleeping. Besides helping keep you warmer, clothing prevents perspiration dried on your skin from infiltrating the bag and promoting the growth of destructive mildew.

▲ Always spread any bag out to air dry for a few hours after a trip; even when it doesn't seem damp, there is moisture inside from your body.

▲ Never store a bag in its stuff sack at home; long-term compression crushes insulation fibers, reducing the bag's loft and warmth. Store it in a breathable sack—many high-end bags come with bulky cotton storage bags—in a dry place away from a heat source and out of direct sunlight.

▲ Only launder a bag if it's smelly or dirty. Better to prevent the accumulation of mildew and dirt through the methods laid out earlier, and postpone laundering for as long as possible, because washing a bag can reduce its loft, especially with down bags. If you do launder a bag, first get the manufacturer's recommendations for washing (often available at the company's website, by calling its customer-service number, or through the retailer where you purchased the bag). Many suggest using front-loading commercial washing machines that don't have an agitator (which can damage the fill) and a mild powder detergent or down soap. Tumble dry on low heat for as many cycles as necessary to dry it thoroughly.

Pad

Besides your bag, the other important component in keeping warm while sleeping outside, especially in winter, is your pad. A pad provides critical insulation between your body and the frozen ground, without which the ground would quickly draw away precious body heat. Because pads are much less expensive than bags, it makes more sense economically to buy a good pad or two and a decent bag than to put all of your money into a top-notch bag while settling for a mediocre pad.

There are numerous models of pads on the market. Traditional closed-cell foam pads are the most lightweight and inexpensive, do not absorb water, and aren't easily damaged, though they offer minimal comfort on a hard ground. Self-inflating pads are more comfortable but heavier and more expensive than foam pads. Specialized models such as down air mattresses are inflatable air mats filled with down to increase their insulation.

As with any gear, your choice of a pad or pads depends on where you're going and your comfort preferences. Camping on snow, which is a fairly soft surface, means comfort isn't usually an issue: Sometimes one thick, full-length foam pad—thick for insulation—is all you need on snow. However, many winter campers use two pads for the added insulation against frozen ground or snow. Think about the combination of pads that makes most sense for you and that incorporates any pad(s) you already own. The lightest, practical two-pad setup would be one three-quarter-length foam pad atop a full-length foam pad (or for tall people, one full-length atop a long pad), providing extra insulation for your head and torso and enough for your feet, where you can use other clothing and gear to boost insulation. For more comfort without adding much weight, combine a three-quarter-length self-inflating pad with a full-length foam pad.

To guarantee a long life for your pad, follow these guidelines:

▲ Allow a self-inflating mattress to self-inflate on its own as much as it will before firming it up with a few breaths. The moisture in your breath can collect inside the pad and freeze during your trip, making the pad colder, and it may thaw and promote the growth of mildew.

▲ Carry an air mat in a stuff sack and have a patch kit handy, because they inevitably spring a leak.

▲ Store a self-inflating air mat unrolled with its valve open.

▲ Thoroughly dry any type of pad and store it in a dry place out of direct sunlight.

▲ Never leave any pad sitting in a car window or where it could be exposed to high heat, which melts foam.

Bivy Bag

A **bivy bag** is a shell bag, waterproof and usually breathable, that you slide a sleeping bag inside in lieu of bringing a tent. Some bivy bags have a small pole or other minimal structure at their head to elevate the shell fabric off your face, and they close up completely to keep out wet weather. A lightweight, portable, and compact shelter, a bivy bag is also minimalist and generally reserved for emergencies or as shelter for a night or two when you're willing to sacrifice comfort to travel lightly. It's not a pleasant shelter for multiple nights, or to wait out stormy weather, because it's claustrophobic and condensation can collect in those close quarters.

Day hikers who want minimalist emergency protection from wind and weather in case of an unplanned, emergency bivouac outside in winter might opt for a bivy bag and a compact sleeping bag.

Stove and Fuel

On multi-day winter trips, a stove is elevated from a convenience to a necessary piece of safety gear. It may provide your only source of water and the hot drink and meal that warms up someone teetering toward hypothermia. Campfires are impractical to rely on for melting snow or cooking in frigid temperatures. On longer trips, consider bringing a second stove in case one fails.

There are basically four types of stoves: canister stoves, alcohol stoves, wood stoves, and liquid-fuel stoves, commonly called "white-gas stoves" in this country because white gas is the preferred fuel type. There are also models that can burn both liquid fuels and canister fuels. In temperatures below freezing, the only real choice is a liquid-fuel stove. Although some newer canister stoves burn more efficiently in cold than older models because they use fuel with a higher ratio of propane to butane, they are not reliable enough to depend on in winter. Alcohol stoves will function in deep cold but are almost excruciatingly slow to boil water, and the colder the air, the slower the boil, which can seriously hinder melting snow for drinking and cooking water. Wood is not a reliable fuel source in winter.

Liquid-fuel stoves burn white gas (for example, Coleman brand gas), and some models burn other fuels like kerosene and automobile gas, which is helpful when traveling overseas where white gas is often unavailable. These stoves typically require setup: attaching a fuel bottle, pressurizing the fuel with a pump, and priming the burner before lighting. They crank out heat even in the deepest cold and strong winds and can boost your spirits at the end of a cold, hard day.

Liquid-fuel stove models differ somewhat in weight, performance, and flame control. One model that's been a winter workhorse for many years is MSR's XGK Expedition. Companies are always improving stoves; check *Backpacker* magazine for current reviews and ask other winter campers and employees at your favorite gear retailer what they recommend.

If you have a problem with a liquid-fuel stove flaring up, it's usually from over-priming. Prime fuel into the burner cup for just a few seconds and then close the fuel valve. Light that primed fuel and let it nearly burn away, until the yellow flame barely licks at the burner, before slowly opening the fuel valve to bring up a uniform blue flame If a yellow flame flares up, turn down the fuel valve. If your liquid-fuel stove is a model that doesn't simmer, reduce the flame by under-pressurizing the fuel bottle or using a heat-deflecting plate when cooking.

Liquid-fuel stoves do require more maintenance than other types. For starters, burn white gas whenever possible—it's cleaner than other fuels. Always carry a maintenance kit. Learn how to disassemble and clean the fuel line, lube or replace the O-ring, and clean the jet while at home, when your fingers are warm. Always clean and fire up your stove before any trip.

Cookware

Use the cook pots and utensils you use at any other time of year. There's little about cookware that requires special equipment or attention in winter, with one exception: When cooking atop snow, a stove must sit atop a firm base to avoid slowly sinking down into the snow (which usually results in the stove or pot tipping over). Affordable metal stove bases that weigh just ounces and fold up into a compact package are sold commercially and work great. An old automobile license plate works just as well (and doubles as a primitive camp shovel), although it's heavier than a stove base. A piece of an old foam pad will work for a while, though the stove heat will eventually melt it.

A second item that's lightweight and conserves at least its weight in white gas—and much more on longer trips—is an Outback Oven (made by Backpacker's Pantry). This heat-reflecting tent fits over a cook pot sitting atop a stove and is used to bake foods in the backcountry (the foods come in mixes—you add water). The oven's benefit is reduced fuel consumption because heat is contained around the pot rather than dispersing as quickly into the air. How much it cuts down your fuel consumption depends on what you're cooking, how much you have to run the stove to melt snow for water, ambient temperature, and other factors, but I'd estimate that you can reduce fuel consumption by 25 percent.

How Much to Carry While Winter Camping

Deciding what to bring and what to leave at home gets a little trickier in winter than in warmer months, because of the greater imperative to carry emergency clothing in winter. In summer, we learn to leave behind clothing and gear that we find ourselves rarely, or never, using (other than the first-aid kit). In winter, you can't apply that rule.

Still, you can apply a looser interpretation of that rule in choosing your clothing for winter camping. How much clothing you need to stay warm depends on your own tolerance for cold and how cold it gets, and it's unwise to fail to bring

Deciding what to carry is a delicate balancing act between being prepared for anything and keeping your load as light as possible so you can move quickly and safely.

enough warm duds for the coldest temperatures you could encounter. With careful scrutiny of your outdoor wardrobe, you may find you rarely or never wear a particular insulating layer and can eliminate it or that you can pare one or more items by substituting with combinations of other garments that you either wear frequently or consider mandatory. And watch the forecast: When it calls for relatively mild temperatures and you consider the forecast reliable, you can probably safely trim back your wardrobe.

Similarly, gear needs vary depending on the trip length, time distance from civilization, and the severity of the terrain and weather. Choose cautiously, but on a short trip, for instance, the backup stove may be unnecessarily superfluous (especially if you test your primary stove at home right before the trip). You also might consider foregoing the tent for a snow shelter or bringing only a lightweight tent that provides overhead shelter, like a rainfly or tarp, and using snow as your floor.

Chapter 9

Eat More; Drink More

Indulge me a personal anecdote: On a 7-day backcountry ski tour in the Bechler Canyon area of Yellowstone National Park, two friends and I planned dinners and daytime meals and snacks amounting to almost twice as much food as we'd have brought if doing the same route in summer. Then I threw into my pack a few extra large-size chocolate bars and a sizable bag of chocolate-peanut clusters. And I ate it all.

If I ate like that for a week at home, even assuming I hit the gym at least a few times, I would have probably put on three pounds. On that Yellowstone trip, I figure I lost ten pounds. We'd had a strenuous week in Yellowstone, with day after day of hard trail breaking in deep powder. However, there are few "easy" trips when you're moving, living, and sleeping in winter conditions day after day. As I wrote in Chapter 3, winter hiking and camping becomes a weight-loss program even when you're making your best effort to put on weight. This chapter sets out to build the house of knowledge that keeps you warm while staying outside for multiple days and nights.

Eat More . . .

In Chapter 3, I estimated that a 35-year-old woman who's 5 feet, 5 inches tall and weighs 130 pounds, hiking uphill for 4 hours with a pack weighing 10 to 20 pounds, in temperatures below freezing, will burn more than 2400 calories. A 5-foot, 9-inch man weighing 150 pounds, carrying the same pack on the same hike, will burn about

When planning food for a multi-day winter trip, expect your food consumption to double compared with a normal day at home.

3000 calories. Those numbers begin to give an idea of how hard we're working when we hike in winter. Add another 2 to 4 hours or more of hard exertion, and you can see how quickly your body's energy needs add up in freezing temperatures.

But those estimates assumed the people in those hypothetical scenarios are day hiking. Those hikers returned afterward to their hypothetical heated homes and—hypothetically, anyway—ate big dinners and rested in a climate-controlled environment that allowed their bodies to truly rest.

On a multi-day backcountry trip in winter, there's no heated home after the hike. Your body continues working even as you sit around the campsite, burning up energy simply to keep warm. The proper clothing helps you stay warm, of course. But the colder it is, the more energy your body will expend generating heat. And it will have to keep working through the night as you sleep and the next morning when you wake up and crawl out of your bag.

Experienced winter campers know well the increased need for food and fluids because their energy demands are something they can physically *feel*. At times during a hike, or after you stop hiking and are sitting around the campsite, you may feel suddenly cold and/or weary and lethargic; but soon after eating and drinking something, you start to feel energized again. Your body tells you when it needs fuel and reacts, noticeably and quickly, to you refilling the tank.

Whether you try to extrapolate the calorie math or learn from the experience of many nights in the winter backcountry, I think you'll reach the same conclusion that I have from many years of being out there: You can't eat too much food on a multi-day backcountry trip in winter. You'll have trouble just eating enough to meet what your body uses. You'll eat frequently just to play calorie catch-up and likely not be able to consume as much as your body burns on the trip. If you spend several hours per day moving, and nighttime low temperatures drop well below freezing, your body may burn 5000 to 7000 calories per day. Look at the nutrition information on the food you plan to pack in, and you'll begin to understand the challenge of eating that much.

When planning food for a multi-day winter trip, count the daily calories, striving for an appropriate balance between carbohydrates, fat, and protein. Find ways to consume more calories, especially calories of carbohydrates and fat: The former provides the quick energy needed during exertion or when you feel hungry or chilled; the latter provides the long-term energy that keeps you warm through the night. Be creative. Add butter to meals. Eat a lot of cheese, chocolate, nuts, yogurt raisins, peanut butter, and jerky, which are easy to chow down on the trail. Once you've planned out your food, throw in extra snacks that you'll enjoy and are high in carbohydrates and fat.

. . . And Drink More

And you certainly cannot drink too much water. It's an old axiom that an adult will exhale a liter of water in his or her breath during a night of sleeping outside in freezing temperatures. After a day of hiking, snowshoeing, or ski touring, down at least a liter of water to prepare yourself to lose that much in your sleep. We often end a day of hiking somewhat dehydrated, even if we've been diligent about drinking frequently. When camping outside, it's more difficult to erase that hydration deficit because you're losing so much moisture in your breath to the cold, dry air, even when not exerting. A conscious effort to drink enough fluids in the evening is required. A few ways to accomplish that include the following:

▲ As soon as you stop for the day, take a long drink and keep your water bottle or hydration pack close by as you set up camp, drinking from it every 15 minutes or so.

▲ While others are putting up the tent and handling other chores, have one party member immediately assume the task of firing up the stove to boil water (or melt snow) for hot drinks or soup—a welcome appetizer or thirst quencher as the air temperature drops.

▲ Later in the evening, before bedtime, fire up the stove again for another round of hot drinks, which will warm everyone's belly, help hydrate them for the night, and provide an avenue for consuming more valuable calories via a sugary powder drink mix like hot cocoa.

▲ Even when you're tired in the evening, be sure to melt enough snow or treat enough backcountry water to have at least one liter per person when you retire for the night, and keep your water nearby to drink during the night when you (inevitably) wake up to pee. (A hot-water bottle or hot drink in your bag keeps it handy and you warm; see Chapter 10.)

▲ In the morning, you'll wake up dehydrated. Try to consume a liter of fluid before hitting the trail, through a combination of hot drinks (noncaffeinated, because caffeine is a diuretic that makes you urinate, contributing to dehydration), hot foods prepared with water, and drinks from your bottle as you pack up.

Cooking Snow

On many multi-day winter trips, backcountry water sources will be solidly frozen and possibly also buried under deep snow. For drinking and cooking water, you'll have to rely on melting snow and maybe ice in a cook pot over a camp stove. Fortunately, in winter, water is everywhere.

Cooking snow for water is as simple as it sounds. To make it go a bit faster, and avoid scorching your pot, start with a half-inch of water in the pot and get it steaming before you start dumping in snow. For efficiency, always replace the pot lid tightly when not adding snow to the pot, and shield your stove and pot from wind as much as possible. An Outback Oven aids fuel efficiency (see Chapter 8).

Fuel consumption skyrockets when you're cooking snow for all of your water. It's difficult to estimate how much fuel you'll need because it depends on the water content of the snow, what you're eating, how well you shield the stove from wind, the ambient air temperature, and how careful you are to not waste fuel. Don't leave a stove burning without a pot on it—either have whatever is going next onto the stove ready or turn the stove off. If you're melting clean snow for drinking water (as opposed to boiling water for cooking), you don't need to bring it to a boil to purify it; to conserve fuel, once the snow's melted in the pot, pour it into your water bottle cold (or hot if preferred, but not boiling). The standard guideline, when you'll be

When melting snow for cooking or drinking water, use a windscreen and heat a small amount of water in the pot before adding snow to avoid scorching the pot.

melting snow for all water needs, is 10–11 ounces of white gas per person per day. Plan your fuel conservatively, always taking extra in case of emergency—and because running out of fuel may also mean you're out of water.

Dry, powder snow typical of the Rockies has a low water content—you'll constantly shovel powder into your cook pot and watch it almost instantly disappear into the steaming water without appearing to add much water to the pot. Wet snow typical of mountain ranges closest to the oceans, like the Appalachians, Sierra Nevada, and Cascades, is heavy because of its high water content; a chunk of wet snow may yield one-fifth of its volume in water.

Ice formed from water (such as ice frozen on a creek) has a higher water content than snow; if you can break chunks of ice to melt for water, do it—remembering that water from a creek should be boiled or treated before drinking. Sometimes ice on a creek or lake may be thin enough to break through to get water, and boiling cold water uses less fuel than melting snow.

If you're camped in powder snow, after stomping out a tent platform and letting the packed snow of the platform firm up, excavate blocks of it for cooking; packing snow makes it more dense and thus increases its water content per square inch. Take the snow blocks either from a corner of your tent platform or from the living and cooking area if you dig one out (see Chapter 10).

Snow in a forest often contains conifer needles and everything else that falls out of trees during the winter, and that detritus gets into your water when melting snow. Once the snow has melted in the pot but before it starts rising to a boil, the needles and other detritus will often float and you can skim it off with a mug or spoon if desired.

The Menu

Winter camping presents a paradox when it comes to food that can be both interesting and frustrating. On the one hand, you're camped in a freezer (or at least a refrigerator)—any foods will keep for as long as you're out there, opening up infinite menu choices. (The challenge is preventing foods from freezing; see Chapter 10.) On the other hand, elaborate food preparation may be difficult or impossible in warm gloves or mittens and render ungloved hands numb or worse in frigid temperatures.

Think about the temperatures and conditions you'll encounter and how much work you want to put into food preparation when planning meals for a trip. Fresh vegetables and fruit are a tasty addition to meals, but you may want to avoid fruit that does not endure cold well (like bananas) or that requires wet peeling (like oranges), and definitely do all of your veggie chopping and prep work at home. Meals that require only boiling water are most convenient. You can find a happy balance between convenience and taste by using grocery store rice, pasta, and bean meals that require only boiling water as a base and adding chopped or dried vegetables, spices, sauces, and canned meat or fish. Keep in mind that fresh produce is heavier than freeze-dried food. Check out some of the good books on backcountry cooking (see Appendix B).

Temperatures comparable to a refrigerator or freezer allow you to bring virtually any food on a multi-day trip—including the fondue these campers ate in Idaho's Sawtooth Mountains.

Chapter 10

The Campsite

T he campsite is the locus of much of the joy of camping in the backcountry in winter. With a snow-covered ground, we have many more potential campsites from which to choose and an opportunity for tremendous creativity in constructing our temporary living quarters. With a little skill and luck, we can enjoy an evening of rarely matched quiet and solitude and a soul-stirring view of wilderness cloaked in white. On winter's long nights, the campsite is where we spend much of our waking time relaxing with companions, eating (and eating, and eating), and engaging in the age-old form of communication too often absent from our lives back in civilization: conversation.

Take the time to find a good campsite in winter. Given the long nights, you'll spend many hours there, and a poorly sited camp can be uncomfortable, whereas a well-chosen site may produce the most lasting memories of the trip.

The Perfect Spot

In many respects, finding the "perfect campsite" is easier with the ground covered with snow than it is in summer: No searching for a flat spot—you can level sloping snow. No hidden rocks and roots under your pad—they're buried. No worrying about locating near a water source—the snow all around is your water source.

That said, these are things to avoid in choosing your camp:

▲ For starters, be aware of and respect all backcountry camping regulations, and

A high campsite with a view, such as this one on Mount Shuksan in Washington's North Cascades, is a treat as long as you don't encounter severe wind.

know how to recognize and avoid avalanche hazard in the mountains.

▲ If you like the view from an exposed ridge or mountaintop, be sure you're confident of a calm night, because those spots tend to get buffeted by strong winds that can damage your tent or keep you awake all night.

▲ Whenever possible, pitch your tent out of the wind, or with its lower end pointing into the wind and the door away from the wind. Sometimes it's possible to camp on the lee side of a broad ridge without getting onto a slope that could possibly avalanche and enjoy a nice view without getting hammered by wind.

▲ Avoid the lowest ground in the area, such as a valley bottom—the coldest air will settle there overnight. Atop a knoll protected by trees is best.

▲ Consider your campsite in the context of a storm: Will you be able to leave safely if a lot of snow fell overnight and slopes at certain angles and aspects suddenly became prone to avalanche?

▲ If there's any concern about animals raiding your food, identifying a proper spot for overnight food storage (such as a tree with a good branch for bear-bagging) should be a priority in selecting your campsite.

Making Camp

Once you've selected a campsite, the real work—and creativity—begins. How you set up camp will affect the rest of your time there. Think about the type of camp you want and how to make it comfortable, given your environment. Some ideas for camping with a tent follow:

▲ At the outset, unless the snow underfoot is firm enough to support your weight without postholing in, you'll have to stomp out a snow platform. Wearing your skis or snowshoes, walk back and forth across an area big enough for your tent plus surrounding area where you want to walk in boots or booties (that is, without putting on snowshoes or skis)—usually, an area about twice the footprint of your tent. During this time, also stomp out a path to your designated "bathroom" (usually a tree or trees nearby) and your food-storage spot if the latter will be separate from your campsite.

▲ In dry powder it can take an hour or more of stomping and waiting for the snow to firm up before it holds your weight without skis or snowshoes. But the snow will eventually firm up and freeze into a solid platform, unless you're in unbonded "sugar" snow, which resembles its nickname and resists packing into snowballs or a firm platform. If that's the case, you might want to relocate. Although sugar snow can cover a large area, sometimes getting to a spot with a different aspect, snow depth, or exposure to sun and wind will yield better snow.

▲ Build a snow wall on the upwind side of your tent as a windbreak or all around your tent if the wind could shift (Illustrations 10-1 and 10-2). It has to be close to the tent to be effective. If winds are severe and you cannot find a spot

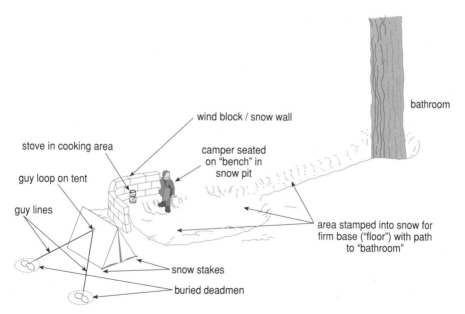

Illustration 10-1: The complete winter campsite features a firm platform stomped into the snow; a path stomped to the "bathroom"; a cooking area protected from wind by a snow wall; and a tent secured by guy lines, stakes, and deadmen.

Illustration 10-2: When camping in strong wind, encircle your tent with a snow wall and pitch your tent with its foot facing into the prevailing wind so you can cook in the lee of your tent while lying inside, out of the wind. (From Cox, Steven M., and Kris Fulsaas, eds. *Mountaineering: The Freedom of the Hills.* 7th ed. Seattle: The Mountaineers Books, 2003.)

protected from them, dig out a tent site a couple feet down into the snow before you begin stomping a platform; this will give you more of a snow wall on all sides as a shield against the wind.

▲ Excavate a living room/kitchen in the snow outside your tent door that's big enough for everyone to sit inside (depending on circumstances, this may be immediately outside your door or a short distance away in a spot that's either more protected or has a better view).

▲ Immediately outside your tent door or vestibule door, cut down 12 to 18 inches into the snow to create a step where you can sit to put on boots or just sit partly protected by the tent.

▲ Mark off in the snow the area for the living room/kitchen. Measuring about a foot in from its edges, dig down a foot or two (how deep you go depends on how hard you want to work vs. how much protection from wind you're seeking) to create a bench around the pit's perimeter. Then dig out the pit's interior floor, about a foot deeper than the bench.

▲ Build a snow windbreak on the upwind side of the pit.

▲ Customize other features such as a cooking surface on the bench or rim of the living room/kitchen, including a snow windbreak for your stove, and small "cabinets" dug into the walls of the pit for storing cooking gear and—if there's no concern about animals—food. You can seal up those cabinets with a block of packed snow the right size to place at the mouth of the cabinet, to prevent contents from being buried by new snowfall or freezing.

Stabilizing Your Tent

Strong winds and heavy snowfall can put tremendous stresses on your tent. Even when the evening starts out clear and calm, stake and guy your tent out securely.

Digging a "kitchen" area snow pit with a shelf for cooking—as long as the air is calm—makes meal preparation more comfortable.

I've had a sturdy winter tent flattened by wind during the night after neglecting to guy it out because the evening began calm.

When pitching a tent in strong wind, make sure it doesn't blow away. Before placing the poles, have one or more persons hold the tent flat to the ground while the others stake out the upwind end of the tent securely. Then stake out the rest of the tent before attaching it to the poles. Attach the rainfly the same way you pitched the tent, with at least one person holding onto it while another attaches the upwind end first.

Three-season tent stakes are too thin to gain purchase in snow; you'll need snow stakes (see Chapter 8). In dry powder or unconsolidated snow, even snow stakes may not hold if planted at the usual slight angle to the ground surface (and tilting slightly away from the tent). If so, use skis, poles, and/or sticks if they're available to stick out the tent corners and ends. If using a ski with metal edges as a stake, turn the ski so that a flat side is against the outer part of the tent's stake loop; if the nylon loop pulls directly against a ski edge, it may slice through the loop.

To all remaining stake loops and guy lines, tie **deadmen,** using snow stakes, rocks, sticks, snowballs, or stuff sacks filled with snow, and bury them in the snow with the guy line or stake loop taut. The deadmen may be prone to immediately pull up out of unconsolidated snow; you may have to spend several minutes standing on the snow above each buried deadman and packing it down with your boots until the deadman holds. I've never seen a deadman pulled up by wind once the snow has set up—they freeze so firmly into place during the evening that they require some effort, kicking at the snow, to remove the next morning.

Cooking

It's safer and more scenic to do all of your cooking outside the tent—and you avoid exacerbating a condensation problem in your tent by boiling water in your vestibule. No matter where you're cooking, shield the stove from wind as much as possible. A stove should come with a windscreen that helps direct its heat to the pot. An Outback Oven concentrates heat around the pot, improving fuel efficiency. You'll also need a stove base to keep the stove from slowly sinking into the snow, which can result in your pot tipping over.

If bad weather forces you to cook inside the vestibule, know how to light your stove to prevent it from flaring up (see Chapter 8). Make sure your tent and vestibule ventilate well enough to prevent the buildup of carbon monoxide, a colorless, odorless, and deadly gas given off by burning fuel. Build a snow wall along the upwind side of the vestibule where the rainfly meets the snow-covered ground (provided you have adequate ventilation elsewhere).

In a tent with an adequately roomy vestibule—a must in winter—there should be no reason to cook inside the tent itself; if you must cook inside,

When done safely, cooking in a vestibule allows you to stay warm and dry inside your tent.

restrict it to the vestibule. Cooking in the tent increases the risks of carbon monoxide poisoning as a result of inadequate ventilation, setting the tent on fire, burning someone, and spilling a pot of water or food on important gear like sleeping bags.

Lastly, learn to light your stove and perform other cooking-related chores with gloves on (without melting your gloves' fingertips). It's a valuable skill on cold trips.

Staying Warm at Night

In those four words—*staying warm at night*—resides all that separates winter hikers from winter campers. The hours between when you stop hiking, snowshoeing, or skiing for the day and when you hit the trail again the next morning are the most challenging time to stay warm because you are no longer producing heat through exertion. Actually, if you have a good sleeping bag, you should be warm enough while inside it. It's the evening hours before crawling into your bag, and the morning hours between when you emerge from the bag and begin moving on the trail again, that demand all of your skills at keeping yourself warm.

In addition to the fundamentals of warmth, other techniques for staying warm in camp include the following:

▲ Get acclimated to cold. I maintain that if you sleep outside in early winter, you'll never feel cold again, anytime, for the rest of that winter, and I think there's at least a nugget of truth in there. Turn down your home thermostat a couple of degrees, and walk around town in a lighter jacket than you're accustomed to wearing. Famed mountaineer Reinhold Messner took cold showers to prepare for high-altitude climbs. Getting accustomed to frigid temperatures can increase production of hormones that boost heat production and train your body to continue sending blood to your extremities even when they feel cold. Many people who spend a lot of time outside in winter will attest to the body's ability to adjust to cold. But do it smartly and safely—don't go so far as to expose your skin to frigid temperatures or water.

▲ Fatten up. Put on a couple extra pounds before an outing of a few days in subfreezing temperatures, or several pounds for an extended trip. You'll burn it off before getting home again, and the fat will help keep you warm.

▲ Think warm. Explorers and adventurers who've endured extreme cold often attest to the power of positive thinking—of telling yourself that you can stay warm and not worrying about being cold. Some have reported successfully concentrating on cold fingers and other extremities to warm them. At the least, positive thinking is more likely to prod you to find a solution to feeling cold rather than being miserable and doing nothing about it.

▲ As much as possible, make efforts during the day to keep outerwear and insulating layers dry, so that they're more effective at keeping you warm *and* so that you don't need to dry them out in the tent or inside your bag at night. Your body is remarkably efficient at drying clothing; by moderating your pace, or layering on the damp clothing during rest breaks, you'll go far in drying it out. If you dry out your shell jacket, for instance, change into the damp fleece while still moving (as long as it doesn't make you overheat or cold), so that both are dry when you reach camp. The cooler temperatures of late afternoon are an ideal time to dry out clothing because you can wear it without overheating. About 15 to 30 minutes before stopping at a campsite for the night, slow your pace so that you're warm but not sweating, and your body heat will dry out the clothing you're wearing. Because your exertion level and body heat production are much lower in camp, it's harder to dry clothing then than it is during the day.

▲ If any clothing—whether a base, insulating, or outer layer—is damp when you reach campsite, change into a dry base and pull the damp one over it; then pull on a dry insulating layer, and pull damp insulating and outer layers over that. You'll stay warm and body heat will dry that stuff before bedtime.

▲ On reaching the campsite, do two things first: eat a big chocolate bar, chunk of cheese, or something similar, and fire up the stove to melt snow for hot drinks or soup.

▲ If your feet are cold at the end of the day, take off your cold boots and socks and warm your bare feet inside your bag before putting on dry socks and footwear. It can help to place a bare foot against the inside of your thigh (one foot at a time).

▲ Be diligent about keeping snow out of the tent and your bags and about ventilating the tent as much as you can short of getting cold.

▲ Don't expose bare hands to extreme cold—but just as importantly, never, ever put cold gloves on hands or cold socks or boots on feet. That will immediately cause vasodilation, and it'll take forever for your body to warm up your hands or feet again. Always warm gloves and socks inside the clothes on your body before putting them on. In the morning (if not overnight), long before you get up, pull the clothing you're going to wear and your boot liners inside your bag with you to warm them up before putting them on. (Boots with removable liners are best because you can leave the snowy shells in the vestibule, and warm the dry liners in your bag without introducing moisture to your bag.)

▲ Insulate your body from the ground. When sitting around camp, sit on a closed-cell foam pad. When lying in the tent, have two pads underneath you or supplement for a second pad with a pack.

▲ If you have chronic problems with cold hands and feet, try some of the chemical hand and foot warmer packets available commercially.

▲ Lay out your bag at least an hour before bedtime to let it loft.

▲ Use a bag liner. Inexpensive liners boost a bag's rating by ten degrees or more.

▲ Lay everyone's pads side by side, close together, to take advantage of the collective warmth of many bodies.

▲ Before crawling into your bag for the night, do jumping jacks, take a walk, or do crunches in your bag to warm your bag quickly.

▲ When sleeping, place a fleece jacket, pack, or anything dense under your feet for added insulation.

▲ Dress right. Keep an extra base layer of clothing dry in your pack to change into at the campsite and wear to bed. In your bag, at a minimum, wear a hat (or two head layers), socks, and a synthetic, wicking base layer—a "boundary" layer against the skin reduces convective and evaporative heat loss. Some people say sleep naked in your bag, others say wear as much clothing as necessary. I say experiment and find what works for you—and understand heat-transfer theory: Insulation traps body heat, whether that insulation is in the form of a thicker bag or layers of breathable clothing worn in the bag. But don't overdress. Besides feeling too constricted to be comfortable, wearing extra clothing in a bag begins to work against you when your extremities become thermally isolated and do not benefit from the body core's heat.

▲ Bring a bottle filled with hot water into your sleeping bag and warm your hands, feet, and core against it.

▲ If your bag is roomy, stuff extra dry clothing around you.

▲ If bears or other animals aren't a concern, keep some high-energy food handy for midnight snacking.

▲ A bag may accumulate moisture each night from your body and external sources like tent condensation, which can reduce its loft—especially a down bag's loft. Counter that by carrying your bag in a waterproof stuff sack (or line a standard nylon sack with a trash bag), drying out your bag whenever you get some sunshine, and wearing more clothes to bed.

▲ When nature calls, don't hold it. Keeping fluid at body temperature uses up energy better spent warming your body. A pee bottle can save you a chilly trip outside during the night.

▲ Finally, don't be proud. If you're cold in camp, get into your bag. If everyone is cold, get into your bags inside the tent—two or three bodies can heat up a small space like a tent interior by as much as ten degrees Fahrenheit warmer (sometimes more) than the outside air temperature. Ditto the next morning: Cook and eat breakfast while cocooned in your bag and/or tent, and load most of your stuff into your pack inside the tent before going outside to break down the tent.

Controlling Condensation and Dampness

Sweat, precipitation, condensation inside your tent and sleeping bag—it seems everything about the winter environment conspires to make you wet. And wet means cold. Therefore, controlling and minimizing dampness in your clothing, tent, and sleeping bag are some of the best preventive methods of staying warm (Illustration 10-3).

To minimize condensation inside a tent, follow these guidelines:

▲ Use a roomy tent and keep snow and precipitation outside.

▲ Always ventilate a tent well by opening vents and doors whenever possible as soon as you get into the tent. If you have a sufficiently warm bag, you shouldn't need to completely close up the tent unless temperatures drop far below zero or a storm rages.

▲ Keep tent doors wide open during hours when you don't need them closed for warmth or weather protection.

▲ Cook in the vestibule only when necessary, and ventilate steam out the vestibule door.

▲ When packing up the tent in the morning, shake and brush off frozen condensation. If possible, dry the tent in direct sunlight.

To keep your bag dry, follow these tips:

▲ Avoid brushing against wet or frosted tent walls.

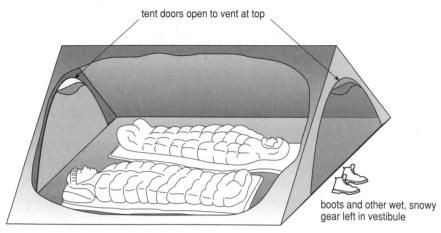

tent doors open to vent at top

boots and other wet, snowy gear left in vestibule

campers careful to keep snow out of tent

Illustration 10-3: To stay warmer, keep your tent interior dry by minimizing condensation and leaving wet items in the vestibule.

▲ Zip your shell jacket around the foot of your bag while sleeping.

▲ Avoid breathing into your bag; keep a small air hole in the hood open over your nose and mouth.

▲ If condensation inside the tent is dripping, try wiping it off the tent fabric with a cloth.

▲ Brush frost off your bag before stuffing it.

▲ Use a bag with a water-resistant or waterproof shell.

▲ Store your bag in a waterproof stuff sack or line a standard nylon stuff sack with a plastic trash bag.

▲ Whenever possible, lay your bag out in the sun to dry.

▲ Don't attempt to dry excessively wet clothing or boots inside your bag at night.

To keep your clothes dry, try these tips:

▲ In the last 30 minutes or so before making camp, pace yourself so that you stay warm without sweating; this will dry out your base layers and, unless wet precipitation is falling, your outer layers.

▲ If some clothing remains damp once in camp, change into dry base layers

Getting Up Warm in the Morning

Getting out of your bag in the morning can be one of the coldest times of winter camping. If you haven't slept with your base and insulating clothing, pull them into your bag to warm them up (including socks, gloves, and boot liners), and dress inside your bag. Do crunches in your bag. Consume a hot drink and food while in your bag or soon after emerging from it.

but pull on your damp layers between the dry base and your outer layers, using body heat to dry the damp stuff (as long as this doesn't make you cold).

▲ Place wet head and hand wear (not balled up) inside closed chest pockets of the breathable jacket you're wearing to dry them during the evening.

▲ Bring damp clothing, boots, and/or boot liners inside your bag with you at night. Damp stuff will dry, but wet stuff may not and may transport more moisture into your bag than the bag can release during the night, leaving your bag (undesirably) damp. Decide between drier clothing or a dry bag.

Backcountry Yurts and Cabins

For people who want to adventure in the backcountry in winter but aren't ready to camp in winter, many parts of the country have systems of backcountry yurts and cabins that can be rented by the public. Some are publicly owned and managed, whereas others that are on public land are owned and/or managed privately by clubs and outfitters. The U.S. Forest Service (202-205-8333, www.fs.fed.us) rents cabins inexpensively. Some states manage yurts for rental. Information can be found in outdoor magazines, from outdoor clubs, at outdoor gear stores, and on websites of public agencies websites and regional offices. Condition and size of the facilities, and regulations, vary greatly as do the terrain in which they are located.

Constructing Snow Shelters

A tent will always be easier and faster than a snow shelter and more logical when you're moving camp every day. But when you need an emergency shelter, or you want a sturdy, spacious, and warm multi-day base camp—and to travel lighter—a snow shelter looks pretty good. Bear in mind that an understanding of different snow conditions is important to constructing a safe snow shelter. Please consult your favorite books or online sources, or take a class in recognizing avalanche hazard.

In most situations, you're likely to build either a snow cave, or a *quin-zhee,* also called an *Athapaskan snow house.* They are essentially the same except that the *quin-zhee* requires first piling up enough snow in a mound to dig out a shelter. Where you have deep, light snow, the snow cave is the obvious choice. Where the snowpack is thin or frozen hard, build a *quin-zhee.*

To build a *quin-zhee* large enough for two or three people, first build a mound of snow at least 6 feet high and 7 feet in diameter at its base, using a shovel, snowshoes, cook pot, or as a last resort, your mittened hands (wear warm, waterproof mittens to avoid frostbite). Let the snow set for an hour or more to firm up. Wet snow sets faster than dry snow.

For a snow cave, look on the lee side of ridges, boulders, and fallen trees for a snowdrift at least 6 or 7 feet deep, avoiding terrain that may have avalanche hazard (see Chapter 4).

From that point, constructing a *quin-zhee* is the same as a snow cave.

If you can find one or two dozen sticks about a foot long, plunge them their full length into the top and sides of your snow mound or drift. As you excavate the interior, hitting the sticks will indicate when your roof is about a foot thick, which is ideal. Once completed, you can remove some of the sticks to create air holes.

Digging out a shelter is wet work—wear waterproof shells. Work at a pace that keeps you warm without overheating or sweating heavily. Two people should periodically swap positions—one excavating inside, the other outside removing the snow piled in the doorway by the person inside.

Backcountry yurts and cabins with woodstoves for cooking and heat are available for rental on public lands in many parts of the country. They offer an introduction to multi-day backcountry trips that's more comfortable than tent camping.

Dig a horizontal tunnel 3 feet high and wide straight into the mound or drift. Once the tunnel is at least a foot long, dig at an upward angle. Keep the door lower than the living quarters to trap warm air inside and keep cold air outside. Dig out the interior to create a domed ceiling, and smooth the ceiling as much as possible so that melting snow drains water down the ceiling and walls rather than dripping from the ceiling.

Build interior sleeping platforms, shelves, and places to sit. Lay a tarp or emergency blanket on your snow bed and your sleeping pad and bag atop it. Use packs in the doorway to keep out a draft. Ventilate the shelter with several small holes (by pulling out the sticks) or one hole the width of a fist, especially if you plan to cook in there.

Whatever the outside temperature, the inside temperature remains around freezing. Keep a shovel inside in case overnight snowfall blocks your doorway. When you leave your snow shelter, mark the entrance with something visible in snow so you can find it.

APPENDIX A:
Resources

Federal Public Lands Agencies

National Park Service (NPS), 1849 C Street NW, Washington, DC 20240; 202-208-6843; *www.nps.gov.*

U.S. Forest Service, 201 14th Street SW, Washington, DC 20024; 202-205-8333; *www.fs.fed.us.*

Major Mapmakers

DeLorme; 800-561-5105; *www.DeLorme.com.*

Earthwalk Press; 800-828-6277.

Topo!; 415-558-8700; *http://maps.nationalgeographic.com/topo/.* National Geographic topographic maps.

Trails Illustrated; 800-962-1643; *http://maps.nationalgeographic.com/trails/maps.cfm.*

USGS Map Sales, Federal Center, Box 25286, Denver, CO 80225. See the USGS website, *http://mcmcweb.er.usgs.gov/topomaps,* for a listing of businesses that sell USGS quad maps.

Major Conservation and Hiking Clubs and Organizations

Some of the following clubs provide instruction in winter hiking and camping.

Adirondack Mountain Club (ADK), 814 Goggins Road, Lake George, NY 12845; 518-668-4447 or 800-395-8080; FAX 518-668-3746; *www.adk.org.*

American Hiking Society, 1422 Fenwick Lane, Silver Spring, MD 20910; 301-565-6704; FAX 301-565-6714; *www.americanhiking.org.*

American Rivers, 1025 Vermont Avenue NW, Suite 720, Washington, DC 20005; 202-347-7550; *www.americanrivers.org.*

Appalachian Mountain Club (AMC), 5 Joy Street, Boston, MA 02108; 617-523-0636; *www.outdoors.org.* Chapters throughout the Northeast.

Colorado Mountain Club, 710 Tenth Street, No. 200, Golden, CO 80401; 303-279-3080; FAX 303-279-9690; *www.cmc.org.*

Green Mountain Club Inc., 4711 Waterbury-Stowe Road, Waterbury Center, VT 05677; 802-244-7037; *www.greenmountainclub.org.*

Idaho Conservation League, P.O. Box 844, Boise, ID 83701, or 710 N. 6th Street, 83702; 208-345-6933; *www.wildIDAHO.org.*

Leave No Trace, Inc., 284 Lincoln Street, Lander, WY 82520; 307-335-2213; FAX 307-332-8811; *www.lnt.org.*

National Parks and Conservation Association, 1300 19th Street NW, Washington, DC 20036; 800-628-7275; *www.npca.org.*

The Nature Conservancy (TNC), 4245 N. Fairfax Drive, Suite 100, Arlington, VA 22203-1606; 703-841-5300; *http://nature.org.*

The Sierra Club, 85 Second Street, Second Floor, San Francisco, CA 94105-3441; 415-977-5500; *www.sierraclub.org.*

Southern Utah Wilderness Alliance (SUWA), 1471 South 1100 E, Salt Lake City, UT 84105; 801-486-3161; FAX 801-486-4233; *www.suwa.org.*

The Wilderness Society, 900 17th Street NW, Washington, DC 20006-2596; 800-THE-WILD; *www.wilderness.org.*

Sources for Information and/or Instruction in Backcountry Skills, Including Winter Hiking and Camping, Avalanche Safety, and Wilderness First Aid

National Outdoor Leadership School (NOLS), 284 Lincoln Street, Lander, WY 82520-2848; 307-332-5300; *www.nols.edu.*

Stonehearth Open Learning Opportunities (SOLO), P.O. Box 3150, Tasker Hill, Conway, NH 03818; 603-447-6711; *www.stonehearth.com.*

The U.S. Forest Service National Avalanche Center, *www.avalanche.org,* has national forecasts, information, and links.

Wilderness Medical Associates, RFD 2, Box 890, Bryant Pond, ME 04219; 888-945-3633; *www.wildmed.com.*

Wilderness Medicine Institute of National Outdoor Leadership School (NOLS), 284 Lincoln Street, Lander, WY 82520-2848; 307-332-7800; *http://wmi.nols.edu/.*

APPENDIX B:
Bibliography

Chapter 1: Where to Go, and Chapter 7: Trip Planning

Berger, Karen. *Everyday Wisdom: 1001 Expert Tips for Hikers.* Seattle: The Mountaineers Books/*Backpacker* magazine, 1997.

————. *More Everyday Wisdom.* Seattle: The Mountaineers Books/*Backpacker* magazine, 2002.

Fenton, Mark. *The Complete Guide to Walking for Health, Weight Loss, and Fitness.* Guilford, Conn.: The Lyons Press, 2001.

Musnick, David, and Mark Pierce. *Conditioning for Outdoor Fitness: A Comprehensive Training Guide.* Seattle: The Mountaineers Books, 1999.

Ross, Cindy, and Todd Gladfelter. *A Hiker's Companion: 12,000 Miles of Trail-Tested Wisdom.* Seattle: The Mountaineers Books, 1993.

Schad, Jerry, and David Moser, eds. *Wilderness Basics: The Complete Handbook for Hikers and Backpackers.* 2d ed. Seattle: The Mountaineers Books, 1992.

Soles, Clyde. *Climbing: Training for Peak Performance.* Seattle: The Mountaineers Books, 2002.

Chapter 2: Clothing and Gear, and Chapter 8: Additional Clothing and Gear for Camping

Lindgren, Louise. *Sew and Repair Your Outdoor Gear.* Seattle: The Mountaineers Books, 1989.

Chapter 3: Water and Food, and Chapter 9: Eat More; Drink More

Miller, Dorcas. *Backcountry Cooking: From Pack to Plate in 10 Minutes.* Seattle: The Mountaineers Books/*Backpacker* magazine, 1998.

Prater, Yvonne, and Ruth Dyar Mendenhall. *Gorp, Glop, and Glue Stew: Favorite Foods from 165 Outdoor Experts.* Seattle: The Mountaineers Books, 1981.

Chapter 4: Getting Around

Burns, Bob, and Mike Burns. *Wilderness Navigation: Finding Your Way Using Map, Compass, Altimeter, and GPS.* Seattle: The Mountaineers Books, 1999.

Fleming, June. *Staying Found: The Complete Map and Compass Handbook.* 3d ed. Seattle: The Mountaineers Books, 2001.

Cox, Steven M., and Kris Fulsaas, eds. *Mountaineering: The Freedom of the Hills.* 7th ed. Seattle: The Mountaineers Books, 2003.

Letham, Lawrence. *GPS Made Easy: Using Global Positioning Systems in the Outdoors.* 3d ed. Seattle: The Mountaineers Books, 2001.

McGivney, Annette. *Leave No Trace: A Guide to the New Wilderness Etiquette.* 2d ed. Seattle: The Mountaineers Books/*Backpacker* magazine, 2003.

Parker, Paul. *Free-Heel Skiing: Telemark and Parallel Techniques for All Conditions.* 3d ed. Seattle: The Mountaineers Books, 2001.

Prater, Gene, and Dave Felkley. *Snowshoeing: From Novice to Master.* 5th ed. Seattle: The Mountaineers Books, 2002.

Ross, Cindy, and Todd Gladfelter. *Kids in the Wild: A Family Guide to Outdoor Recreation.* Seattle: The Mountaineers Books, 1995.

Tremper, Bruce. *Staying Alive in Avalanche Terrain.* Seattle: The Mountaineers Books, 2001.

Chapter 5: Weather

Renner, Jeff. *Northwest Mountain Weather: Understanding and Forecasting for the Backcountry User.* Seattle: The Mountaineers Books, 1992.

———. *Renner's Guide to Mountain Weather.* Seattle: The Mountaineers Books, 1999.

Chapter 6: Backcountry Ailments

Steele, Peter. *Backcountry Medical Guide.* 2d ed. Seattle: The Mountaineers Books, 1999.

Tilton, Buck, and Frank Hubbell. *Medicine for the Backcountry: A Practical Guide to Wilderness First Aid.* Guilford, Conn.: The Globe Pequot Press, 1999.

Van Tilburg, Christopher. *Emergency Survival: A Pocket Guide.* Seattle: The Mountaineers Books, 2001.

———. *First Aid: A Pocket Guide.* 4th ed. Seattle: The Mountaineers Books, 2001.

Weiss, Eric. *Wilderness 911: A Step-by-Step Guide for Medical Emergencies and Improvised Care in the Backcountry.* Seattle: The Mountaineers Books/*Backpacker* magazine, 1998.

Wilkerson, James A, ed. *Hypothermia, Frostbite, and Other Cold Injuries: Prevention, Recognition, Prehospital Treatment.* Seattle: The Mountaineers Books, 1986.

Wilkerson, James A, ed. *Medicine for Mountaineering and Other Wilderness Activities.* 5th ed. Seattle: The Mountaineers Books, 2001.

Chapter 10: The Campsite

Meyer, Kathleen. *How to Shit in the Woods.* 2d ed. San Francisco: Ten Speed Press, 1994.

Renner, Jeff. *Lightning Strikes.* Seattle: The Mountaineers Books, 2001.

Rezendes, Paul. *Tracking and the Art of Seeing.* 2d ed. New York: HarperResource, 1999.

Smith, David. *Backcountry Bear Basics: The Definitive Guide to Avoiding Unpleasant Encounters.* Seattle: The Mountaineers Books, 1997.

Tilton, Buck, and Rick Bennett. *Don't Get Sick! The Hidden Dangers of Camping and Hiking.* Seattle: The Mountaineers Books, 2001.

APPENDIX C:
Glossary

Altimeter: A handheld device used to measure altitude, or elevation, above sea level, which is usually obtained by measuring barometric pressure.

Altitude illness, or **acute mountain sickness (AMS):** A physical ailment directly related to being at an altitude at which one's body is not acclimated. Symptoms may occur as low as 8000 feet above sea level, although that varies among individuals. Symptoms may be as nonthreatening as a headache and nausea but can quickly become life threatening, taking forms including high altitude pulmonary edema (HAPE) and high altitude cerebral edema (HACE). Descending to a lower altitude is the only treatment.

Aspect: The particular compass direction a slope faces.

Avalanche: A large volume of snow releasing suddenly and falling rapidly downhill, occurring either spontaneously or triggered by people or animals moving across unstable snow. Avalanches can cover large areas, involve tons of snow, and be fatal for anyone in their path.

Balaclava: A close-fitting garment that fits over the entire head and neck, with a face opening.

Bear-bagging: A technique used to hang food from a tree branch beyond reach of bears and other animals, so that the food is at least 10 feet off the ground, 4 feet from the trunk, and 4 feet below the branch, and sometimes involving counter-balancing two food sacks.

Bivy bag, or **bivouac:** An outer bag, usually waterproof-breathable, inside which you slide your sleeping bag to keep yourself dry and protected from the wind; typically used as shelter in an emergency or for a night or two on a mountain climb.

Calorie: The quantity of heat required to raise the temperature of one gram of pure water by one degree Celsius, or a unit of energy provided by food.

Conductive cooling: When moisture on skin and clothing conducts heat away from the body, accelerating the rate at which the body cools down.

Corona: A tight, bright ring around the moon or sun, which is actually an optical effect created by thin clouds, water droplets, or ice in the atmosphere.

Deadman: Any object, including a tent stake, stick, rock, or stuff sack filled with snow, tied to a tent stake loop or guy line and buried in snow (with the attached line taut) to help stabilize the tent.

Declination: In the context of navigating with a magnetic compass, the angle of difference from a point on the Earth between the direction of true north and the direction of magnetic north, measured in degrees on a circle.

Dehydration: A dangerous lack of water in the body resulting from inadequate intake of fluids or excessive loss through sweating, vomiting, or diarrhea.

Double-wall tent: A tent with a traditional design of a distinct canopy over the tent's interior and a rainfly (that is, two walls).

Durable, water-repellent (DWR) coating: A coating applied to some technical outdoor garments to help them shed water.

Frostbite: Skin tissue cooling or freezing as a result of the loss of circulation to that part of the body.

Gaiters: A garment covering the lower leg from the boot top to just below the knee, usually waterproof and sometimes breathable; low gaiters are cut lower, at calf height.

Global Positioning System (GPS) receiver: An electronic, handheld receiver that picks up signals from satellites to locate one's position on the Earth's surface; it is more precise than is usually possible with a map and compass.

Gore-Tex: Developed by W.L. Gore & Associates, Inc., this fabric membrane is used in outdoor products from jackets to boots because it "breathes"—releases moisture from within—while remaining waterproof and prevents moisture on the outside from penetrating the membrane.

Halo: A wide, bright ring around the moon or sun, which is actually an optical effect created by thin clouds, water droplets, or ice in the atmosphere.

Hook-and-loop: The generic term for what's commonly known as "Velcro" (one brand name), the name originating in the design, which mates tiny hooks on one fabric face to tiny loops on the opposite fabric face.

Hydration system: A marketing euphemism for having drinking water built into a pack. It consists of a hose with a mouthpiece running from a water bladder inside the pack, enabling the wearer to drink without having to stop moving or dig out a water bottle.

Hypothermia: A core body temperature below 95 degrees Fahrenheit (normal is around 98.6 degrees Fahrenheit). It occurs as the body core temperature drops in response to the body losing heat to the environment faster than it can produce heat.

Last: In shoes and boots, the foot mold around which footwear is constructed.

Magnetic north: The Earth's magnetic north pole located in Arctic Canada, south of the North Pole. Magnetic compass needles point to magnetic north rather than true north.

Moat: A trench that forms anywhere there is snow and an object that radiates solar heat (such as a cliff face or large boulder). The trench steadily widens and deepens as snow melts. Moats may be a few feet to several feet across and deeper than they are wide.

Orient: In the context of maps and navigation, the aligning of a map so that directions on it correspond with directions on the ground.

Orographic effect: Wind flowing against, up, and over an isolated peak or an entire mountain ridge.

Postholing: Plunging on foot deeply into snow that's either soft and wet or dry and light.

Quin-zhee, or **Athapaskan snow house:** A snow cave dug out of a prepared mound of snow.

Self-arrest: A technique involving the use of an ice ax or similar tool to stop oneself from sliding out of control down a snow-covered or icy slope.

Single-wall tent: A tent replacing the traditional, separate rainfly and tent canopy with a single wall that is waterproof.

Snow blindness: A sunburn to the cornea typically caused by hours of exposure to bright sunlight on snow with the eyes unprotected. Although usually only a temporary condition, it is debilitating and painful.

Soft shell: A term used to describe a jacket or pant that blocks wind, repels water (such as steady, light rain), is durable and stretchy, dries fast, and breathes well.

Sugar snow, or **T.G. snow:** Unconsolidated snow that cannot be packed and often resembles tiny ball bearings.

Suspension system: In packs, the hipbelt, shoulder straps, and support structure such as a frame sheet and/or stays that support a pack's weight on your back.

True north: The straight-line direction from wherever one is standing to the North Pole.

Wand: A small flaglike item, usually comprised of thin bamboo sticks with a piece of brightly colored nylon or route-marking tape tied to the top, placed upright in the snow at intervals along a route, typically used by climbers to enable them to find their way back down the mountain.

Waterproof-breathable (W-B): A fabric or membrane, commonly used in boots and jackets, that keeps external, environmental water (like rain) out, but allows water vapor (like perspiration) to escape from the inside to the outside.

Whiteout: A disorienting inability to visually distinguish the air from the snow-covered ground, which is usually caused by heavy snowfall or dense fog that blends the milky color of the air seamlessly into the equally milky and featureless ground. It occurs in terrain lacking trees or other vegetation.

Windchill: A measure of the effective temperature, or equivalent temperature, of the combination of a given ambient air temperature and wind speed.

Index

About the Author

The first time freelance writer and photographer Michael Lanza camped in winter—in New Hampshire's famously frigid Presidential Range—the temperature dropped to twenty degrees below zero Fahrenheit. He loved it. Over the past two decades, he has spent innumerable days and nights outside in winter (his coldest was thirty degrees below zero Fahrenheit) from his native New England to his chosen home state of Idaho. Lanza serves as the Northwest editor for *Backpacker* magazine and writes a monthly column and other articles for *AMC Outdoors* magazine. His work has also appeared in *Boys' Life*, *National Geographic Adventure*, *Outside*, and other publications. He is the author of three other books, *Day Hiker's Handbook* (The Mountaineers Books, 2003), *New England Hiking* (Foghorn Press, 3rd edition, 2002), and *The Ultimate Guide to Backcountry Travel* (Appalachian Mountain Club, 1999).

An avid hiker, backpacker, climber, cyclist, and backcountry and skate-skier, Lanza serves as the president of the Boise Climbers Alliance, as the southern Idaho volunteer regional coordinator for The Access Fund, and as an advisor on the board of *AMC Outdoors*. During the mid-1990s he wrote a weekly column about the New England outdoors that was syndicated in approximately twenty daily newspapers throughout the region; he also cohosted an outdoors talk show on New Hampshire Public Radio. A native of Leominster, Massachusetts, Lanza graduated with a bachelor's degree in photojournalism from Syracuse University and spent ten years as a reporter and editor at newspapers in Massachusetts and New Hampshire. He lives in Boise, Idaho, with his wife, Penny Beach, and their son, Nate, and daughter, Alex.

THE MOUNTAINEERS, founded in 1906, is a nonprofit outdoor activity and conservation club, whose mission is "to explore, study, preserve, and enjoy the natural beauty of the outdoors . . . ." The Club sponsors many classes and year-round outdoor activities in the Pacific Northwest, and supports environmental causes through educational activities, sponsoring legislation, and presenting educational programs. The Mountaineers Books supports the club's mission by publishing travel and natural history guides, instructional texts, and works on conservation and history.

Send or call for our catalog of more than 500 outdoor titles:

 The Mountaineers Books
1001 SW Klickitat Way, Suite 201
Seattle, WA 98134
800-553-4453
mbooks@mountaineersbooks.org
www.mountaineersbooks.org

BACKPACKER
THE OUTDOORS AT YOUR DOORSTEP

33 East Minor Street
Emmaus PA, 18098
1-800-666-3434
www.backpacker.com

The mission of *Backpacker* magazine is to provide accurate, useful, in-depth and engaging information about wilderness recreation in North America.

 The Mountaineers Books is proud to be a corporate sponsor of Leave No Trace, whose mission is to promote and inspire responsible outdoor recreation through education, research, and partnerships. The Leave No Trace program is focused specifically on human-powered (nonmotorized) recreation.

Leave No Trace strives to educate visitors about the nature of their recreational impacts, as well as offer techniques to prevent and minimize such impacts. Leave No Trace is best understood as an educational and ethical program, not as a set of rules and regulations.

For more information, visit *www.LNT.org,* or call 800-332-4100.

MORE TITLES IN THE BACKPACKER MAGAZINE SERIES FROM THE MOUNTAINEERS BOOKS:

Trekker's Handbook: Strategies to Enhance Your Journey, *Buck Tilton*
Contains pre-trip, during the trip, and post-trip strategies for long-distance hiking

Everyday Wisdom: 1001 Expert Tips for Hikers, *Karen Berger*
Expert tips and tricks for hikers and backpackers selected from one of the most popular *Backpacker* magazine columns

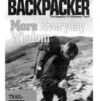

More Everyday Wisdom: Trail-Tested Advice from the Experts, *Karen Berger*
More tips for enhancing backcountry trips

Backcountry Cooking: From Pack to Plate in 10 Minutes, *Dorcas Miller*
More than 144 recipes and how to plan simple meals

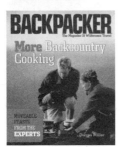

More Backcountry Cooking: Moveable Feasts from the Experts, *Dorcas Miller*
Practical, tasty recipes that are quick, easy, and nutritious

Day Hiker's Handbook: Get Started with the Experts, *Michael Lanza*
Learn how to get started, what gear to choose, and how to handle possible dangers

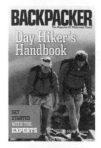

Leave No Trace: A Guide to the New Wilderness Ethic, *Annette McGivney*
Learn how to minimize your impact on the environment and support the LNT Center for Outdoor Ethics

Wilderness 911: A Step-by-Step Guide for Emergencies and Improvised Care in the Backcountry, *Eric A. Weiss, M.D.*

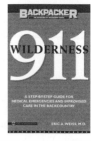

Available at fine bookstores and outdoor stores, by phone at 800-553-4453 or on the Web at *www.mountaineersbooks.org*

THE MOUNTAINEERS BOOKS